PRISM
READING

Student's Book

4

Jessica Williams

with
Christina Cavage

D1599554

CAMBRIDGE
UNIVERSITY PRESS

CAMBRIDGE
UNIVERSITY PRESS

University Printing House, Cambridge CB2 8BS, United Kingdom

One Liberty Plaza, 20th Floor, New York, NY 10006, USA

477 Williamstown Road, Port Melbourne, VIC 3207, Australia

314–321, 3rd Floor, Plot 3, Splendor Forum, Jasola District Centre, New Delhi – 110025, India

79 Anson Road, #06–04/06, Singapore 079906

Cambridge University Press is part of the University of Cambridge.

It furthers the University's mission by disseminating knowledge in the pursuit of education, learning and research at the highest international levels of excellence.

www.cambridge.org
Information on this title: www.cambridge.org/9781108638487

First published 2018
20 19 18 17 16 15 14 13 12 11 10 9 8 7 6 5 4 3 2 1

Printed in Malaysia by Vivar

A catalogue record for this publication is available from the British Library

ISBN 978-1-108-63848-7 Prism Reading 4 Student's Book with Online Workbook
ISBN 978-1-108-45535-0 Prism Reading 4 Teacher's Manual

CONTENTS

SCOPE AND SEQUENCE

UNIT	READING PASSAGES	KEY READING SKILLS	ADDITIONAL READING SKILLS	
1 PRESERVATION *Academic Disciplines* Architecture / Information Technology / Urban Planning	1: Are We Living in the Digital Dark Ages? (article) 2: Build It up or Tear It down? (mixed texts)	Identifying an argument Identifying supporting details	Using your knowledge Previewing Understanding key vocabulary Reading for main ideas Reading for details Annotating Making inferences Skimming Identifying purpose Synthesizing	
2 EDUCATION *Academic Disciplines* Graphic Design / Marketing	1: What Makes a Successful Logo? (textbook excerpt) 2: Rebranding and Logos (textbook excerpt)	Making inferences Using an outline to take notes	Using your knowledge Understanding key vocabulary Previewing Reading for main ideas Taking notes Identifying purpose Reading for details Synthesizing	
3 PRIVACY *Academic Disciplines* Business / Criminal Justice / Media	1: Cyber Harassment (online article) 2: Combatting Cyber Harassment (article)	Previewing Identifying purpose and tone	Understanding key vocabulary Using your knowledge Reading for main ideas Reading for details Taking notes Annotating Synthesizing	
4 BUSINESS *Academic Disciplines* Business / Marketing / Social Media	1: Starting Out Mobile (online article) 2: Keeping Your Customers (article)	Scanning	Using your knowledge Understanding key vocabulary Reading for main ideas Working out meaning Annotating Reading for details Making inferences Synthesizing	

LANGUAGE DEVELOPMENT	WATCH AND LISTEN	SPECIAL FEATURES
Time expressions Compound adjectives	Preserving CDs at the Library of Congress	Critical Thinking Collaboration
Describing emotional responses Paraphrasing	The Role of Helvetica Font in Graphic Design	Critical Thinking Collaboration
Collocations for behavior Problem-solution collocations	Computer Fraud: Celebrity Hacking	Critical Thinking Collaboration
Expressing contrast Business and marketing vocabulary	Florida Teen Buys Houses	Critical Thinking Collaboration

UNIT	READING PASSAGES	KEY READING SKILLS	ADDITIONAL READING SKILLS	
5 PSYCHOLOGY *Academic Disciplines* Experimental Science / History / Neuroscience	1: Mental Illness and Creative Genius: Is There a Connection? (article) 2: The Creative Mind (online article)	Using graphic organizers to take notes Interpreting quotes	Understanding key vocabulary Previewing Taking notes Making inferences Predicting content using visuals Reading for main ideas Reading for details Synthesizing	
6 CAREERS *Academic Disciplines* Business / Education / Information Technology	1: The Skills Gap (report) 2: What Is the Value of Education? (article)	Interpreting graphical information	Understanding key vocabulary Predicting content using visuals Reading for main ideas Reading for details Annotating Identifying purpose and tone Making inferences Synthesizing	
7 HEALTH SCIENCES *Academic Disciplines* Global Studies / Medicine	1: Superbugs (article) 2: The Globalization of Infection (article)	Recognizing discourse organization	Using your knowledge Understanding key vocabulary Reading for main ideas Taking notes Making inferences Scanning to predict content Reading for details Synthesizing	
8 COLLABORATION *Academic Disciplines* Business / Human Resources / Sports Management	1: The Value of Talent (article) 2: The Perfect Work Team: Getting the Best from a Group (article)	Using context clues to understand terminology and fixed expressions	Understanding key vocabulary Previewing Reading for main ideas Summarizing Reading for details Working out meaning Using your knowledge Taking notes	

LANGUAGE DEVELOPMENT	WATCH AND LISTEN	SPECIAL FEATURES
Experimental science vocabulary Complex noun phrases with *what*	Interview with the Founders of IDEO	Critical Thinking Collaboration
Complex noun phrases	Vocational Training	Critical Thinking Collaboration
Verbs and verb phrases for causation Health and medicine word families	Superbugs	Critical Thinking Collaboration
Language for hedging	Office Space	Critical Thinking Collaboration

① READING

Receptive, language, and analytical skills

Students improve their reading skills through a sequence of proven activities. First they study key vocabulary to prepare for each reading and to develop academic reading skills. Then they work on synthesis exercises in the second reading that prepare students for college classrooms. Language Development sections teach vocabulary, collocations, and language structure.

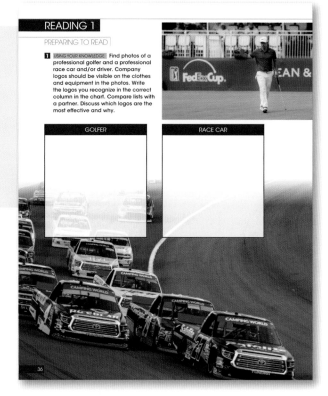

② MORE READING

Critical thinking and collaboration

Multiple critical thinking activities prepare students for exercises that focus on academic reading skills. Collaboration activities help develop higher-level thinking skills, oral communication, and understanding of different opinions. By working with others students, they become better prepared for real life social and academic situations.

③ VIDEO

Summarizing the unit

Each unit ends with a carefully selected video clip that piques student interest and pulls together what they have learned. Video lessons also develop key skills such as prediction, comprehension, and discussion.

PREPARE YOUR STUDENTS TO SUCCEED IN COLLEGE CLASSES AND BEYOND

Capturing interest

- Students experience the topics and expand their vocabulary through captivating readings and videos that pull together everything they have learned in the unit, while developing academic reading and critical thinking skills.

- Teachers can deliver effective and engaging lessons using Presentation Plus.

Building confidence

- *Prism Reading* teaches skills that enable students to read, understand, and analyze university texts with confidence.

- Readings from a variety of academic disciplines in different formats (essays, articles, websites, etc.) expose and prepare students to comprehend real-life text they may face in or outside the classroom.

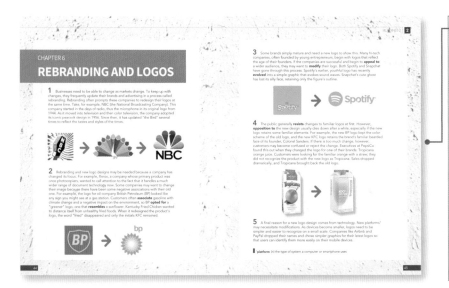

Extended learning

- The Online Workbook has one extra reading and additional practice for each unit. Automated feedback gives autonomy to students while allowing teachers to spend less time grading and more time teaching.

Research-based

- Topics, vocabulary, academic and critical thinking skills to build students' confidence and prepare them for college courses were shaped by conversations with teachers at over 500 institutions.

- Carefully selected vocabulary students need to be successful in college are based on the General Service List, the Academic Word List, and the Cambridge English Corpus.

PATH TO
BETTER LEARNING

CLEAR LEARNING OBJECTIVES

Every unit begins with clear learning objectives.

RICH CONTENT

Highly visual unit openers with discussion questions are engaging opportunities for previewing unit themes.

SCAFFOLDED INSTRUCTION

Activities and tasks support the development of critical thinking skills.

COLLABORATIVE GROUP WORK

Critical thinking is followed by collaborative tasks and activities for the opportunity to apply new skills. Tasks are project-based and require teamwork, research, and presentation. These projects are similar to ones in an academic program.

CRITICAL THINKING

After reading, targeted questions help develop critical thinking skills. The questions range in complexity to prepare students for higher-level course work.

EXTENDED LEARNING OPPORTUNITIES

In-class projects and online activities extend learning beyond the textbook.

BETTER
LEARNING

WHAT MAKES *PRISM READING* SPECIAL: CRITICAL THINKING

BLOOM'S TAXONOMY

Prism Reading prepares students for college coursework by explicitly teaching a full range of critical thinking skills. Critical thinking exercises appear in every unit of every level, organized according to the taxonomy developed by Benjamin Bloom.

Critical thinking exercises are highlighted in a special box and indicates which skills the students are learning.

☼ CRITICAL THINKING

8 SYNTHESIZING **Work with a partner. Use ideas from Reading 1 and Reading 2 to discuss the questions.**

APPLY

Describe your response to a specific logo, and compare it to your partner's.

ANALYZE

Choose one of the pairs of logos discussed in Reading 2. Why do you think the company made the change?

EVALUATE

How important do you think a logo is for a brand? Support your idea with examples.

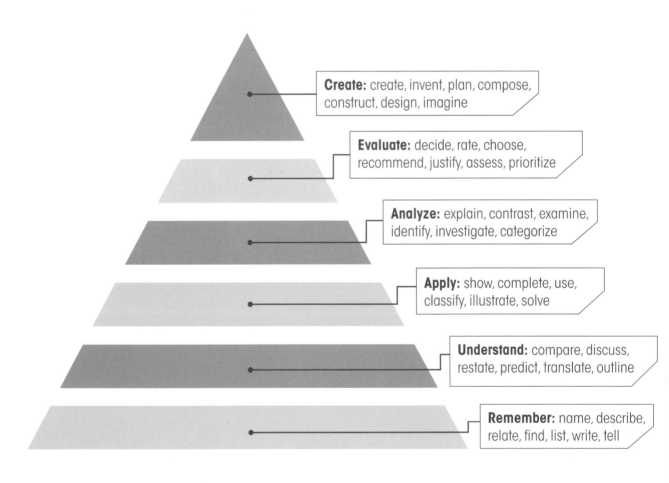

Create: create, invent, plan, compose, construct, design, imagine

Evaluate: decide, rate, choose, recommend, justify, assess, prioritize

Analyze: explain, contrast, examine, identify, investigate, categorize

Apply: show, complete, use, classify, illustrate, solve

Understand: compare, discuss, restate, predict, translate, outline

Remember: name, describe, relate, find, list, write, tell

HIGHER-ORDER THINKING SKILLS

Create, Evaluate, Analyze

Students' academic success depends on their ability to derive knowledge from collected data, make educated judgments, and deliver insightful presentations. *Prism Reading* helps students gain these skills with activities that teach them the best solution to a problem, and develop arguments for a discussion or presentation.

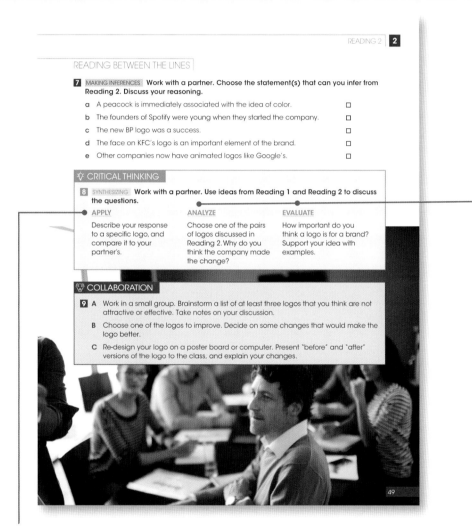

READING 2 | **2**

READING BETWEEN THE LINES

7 MAKING INFERENCES **Work with a partner. Choose the statement(s) that can you infer from Reading 2. Discuss your reasoning.**

a A peacock is immediately associated with the idea of color. ☐

b The founders of Spotify were young when they started the company. ☐

c The new BP logo was a success. ☐

d The face on KFC's logo is an important element of the brand. ☐

e Other companies now have animated logos like Google's. ☐

🔆 CRITICAL THINKING

8 SYNTHESIZING **Work with a partner. Use ideas from Reading 1 and Reading 2 to discuss the questions.**

APPLY

Describe your response to a specific logo, and compare it to your partner's.

ANALYZE

Choose one of the pairs of logos discussed in Reading 2. Why do you think the company made the change?

EVALUATE

How important do you think a logo is for a brand? Support your idea with examples.

🤝 COLLABORATION

9 **A** Work in a small group. Brainstorm a list of at least three logos that you think are not attractive or effective. Take notes on your discussion.

B Choose one of the logos to improve. Decide on some changes that would make the logo better.

C Re-design your logo on a poster board or computer. Present "before" and "after" versions of the logo to the class, and explain your changes.

49

LOWER-ORDER THINKING SKILLS

Apply, Understand, Remember

Students need to be able to recall information, comprehend it, and see its use in new contexts. These skills form the foundation for all higher-order thinking, and *Prism Reading* develops them through exercises that teach note-taking, comprehension, and the ability to distill information from charts.

PRESERVATION

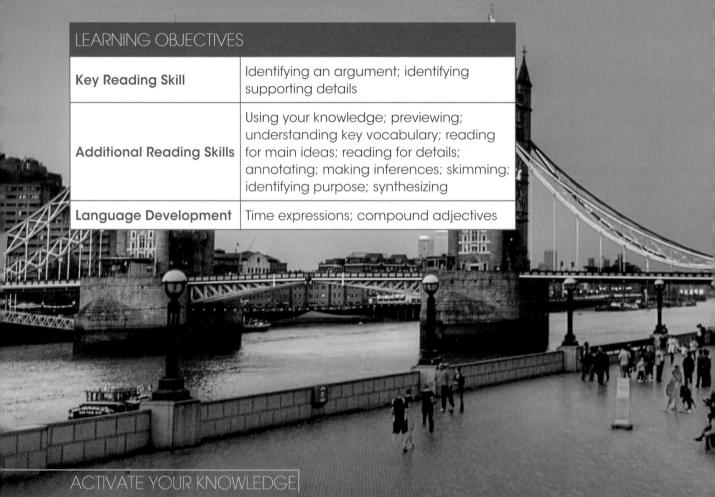

LEARNING OBJECTIVES

Key Reading Skill	Identifying an argument; identifying supporting details
Additional Reading Skills	Using your knowledge; previewing; understanding key vocabulary; reading for main ideas; reading for details; annotating; making inferences; skimming; identifying purpose; synthesizing
Language Development	Time expressions; compound adjectives

ACTIVATE YOUR KNOWLEDGE

Work with a partner. Discuss the questions.

1 Do you like to visit old buildings or museums that show something about our past? Why or why not?

2 Do you like looking at old family photos or old letters and postcards? Who keeps these things? How do they keep them (in photo albums, in a shoebox, in boxes in the attic)?

3 How important is it to preserve the past: buildings, records, art? Is preserving the past more important than creating new things?

PREPARING TO READ

1 USING YOUR KNOWLEDGE You are going to read an article about storing records. Look at the list of information and records—in text, audio, and visual form—about your life. Add four more examples of your own. Then check where you store each type of thing. Compare answers with a partner.

	in a box or drawer	on my phone/ tablet	in the cloud	I throw them away.
old school records				
family photos				
bank statements				
selfies from vacation				
medical records				
receipts from major purchases				
music				

2 PREVIEWING Work with a partner. Discuss the questions.

1 Think about items in the chart in Exercise 1. How long will records last? Will your grandchildren be able to access them? Why or why not?

2 Look at the title of the article on pages 18–19. What does the word *digital* mean there? Give some examples of digital devices that you use. What are some digital devices that are no longer widely used?

3 The *Dark Ages* is a period of European history from about 500 CE to 1000 CE. How do you think it relates to the article?

3 UNDERSTANDING KEY VOCABULARY **Read the sentences and write the words in bold next to the definitions.**

1 The designers of the new phone have made a **deliberate** effort to make the device easy for anyone to use.

2 It is a common **practice** to name a baby after a parent or grandparent.

3 I am upset because my computer crashed and I have not been able to **recover** the files on it.

4 We can't plan for everything, so we will have to handle problems as they **emerge**.

5 Your computer files are **vulnerable** if you don't protect them with a strong password.

6 All of the devices have the **capacity** to update information over Wi-Fi.

7 Problems with security **prompted** software designers to make major changes to the new version of the program.

8 The closet was filled with boxes of **memorabilia** from my childhood and my parents' early years of marriage.

a _____ (adj) not well protected; able to be harmed

b _____ (n) a regular or widespread habit or behavior

c _____ (v) to cause to do something

d _____ (v) to get something back

e _____ (n) ability

f _____ (adj) intentional

g _____ (n) a collection of items connected to a person or event

h _____ (v) to become known

ARE WE LIVING IN THE DIGITAL DARK AGES?

1 Imagine these scenarios: (1) 2040: A box of **memorabilia**, including floppy discs and VHS tapes[1], is found in the attic of an old house with a label that says, "Records and early videos of Bill Gates (1975–1985)." (2) 2050: You find an envelope labeled "bank records" in your grandmother's desk. Inside the envelope, there is an old CD marked with the date 1998, your great-grandfather's name, and the words "all overseas bank accounts."

2 If these stories were really to happen, the people who found these items would be very excited—at least at first. Their excitement would be quickly followed by frustration because it would be very difficult for them to access the information on the discs and tapes. Even if the records were still in good condition, it would be very hard to find a device that could read them. Compare these discoveries to one that might have occurred around the turn of the twentieth century: a box of old letters and photographs on a high shelf at the back of a closet. The information these items contain would be immediately accessible because you would only need your eyes.

3 Computers and digital technology have vastly expanded our **capacity** to store all kinds of information, but how long will our access to this stored information last? In fact, the people who found the discs and tapes in our scenarios would be lucky because discs and tapes are physically real. Information on the Web is much more **vulnerable**; it is completely digital and can disappear in a flash. This is a problem that began to worry technology experts in the early 2000s. They became concerned that, without better ways of preserving information, future generations might look back on our times as the "digital dark ages." If current **practices** continue, future generations may not have access to the digital record of our lives and our world.

4 Vint Cerf, a vice president at Google, argues that this could happen if we do not take steps quickly. He uses the term "bit rot" to describe how our digital records may slowly but surely become inaccessible. In our scenarios, for example, we may no longer have the devices, such as video and CD players, to access the records. Most software and apps that were used to create documents and websites ten or twenty years ago are already out of date, and in another sixty years they may not even be available. The problem is particularly challenging with interactive apps and websites. We can read letters from long ago, but will we be able to read a Twitter feed or access a Snapchat exchange a hundred years from now?

[1] **floppy discs and VHS tapes** (n) early forms of electronic media storage

> **Information on the Web ... can disappear in a flash.**

5 This problem has **prompted** technology experts like computer scientist Mahadev Satyanarayanan of Carnegie Mellon University to take action. He has found a way to store everything that is needed to interpret a record—the record itself as well as the original operating system and the application it used—all together in the cloud. Using this approach, he has been able to **recover** and preserve digital records that might otherwise have been lost forever.

6 Both Cerf and Satyanarayanan stress the importance of **deliberate** preservation. In the past, you could throw a bunch of photos into a box without having to decide what to save and what to throw away. With digital records, however, you need to make an active decision about what to keep. Satyanarayanan says it is likely that important records—government documents, big news stories, etc.—will be transferred to new forms of storage technology as they **emerge**. It is the records of everyday life, the ones we do not yet know we will value, that may disappear into the digital dark ages.

Physical Storage Media
(with approximate date of first use)

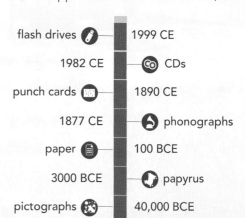

flash drives — 1999 CE

1982 CE — CDs

punch cards — 1890 CE

1877 CE — phonographs

paper — 100 BCE

3000 BCE — papyrus

pictographs — 40,000 BCE

✎ SKILLS

IDENTIFYING AN ARGUMENT

Most academic texts put forth an argument (or *claim*). It is important to be able to identify the central claim in a text and then to locate the evidence that the writer uses to support that argument.

4 READING FOR MAIN IDEAS **Read the article on pages 18–19, and complete the tasks.**

1 Which sentence best captures the writer's central claim?

    a Digital technology is not keeping up with the need to save records.

    b It would be easier to keep records if we made a physical copy of everything.

    c We are not preserving our digital records, so our history may be lost.

    d As our capacity to store records increases, we have to throw more things away.

2 Underline the sentence in the article that expresses this claim.

5 READING FOR DETAILS **Read the article again. Answer the questions with information from the article.**

1 The writer begins with **two** examples to illustrate the central claim. What are they? _____

_____

2 Reread Paragraph 4. What **two** problems with our current practices does Vint Cerf point out?

    a Physical records take up much more space than digital records. ☐

    b The devices necessary to read our records will not be available. ☐

    c Software used to create applications goes out of date quickly. ☐

    d We may not have access to the cloud in the future. ☐

    e It is not possible to preserve interactive applications such as Snapchat and Twitter. ☐

3 Where does Satyanarayanan suggest keeping digital records?

_____

6 ANNOTATING Write **T** (true), **F** (false), or **DNS** (does not say) next to the statements. Highlight the information in the article that helps you decide the answers, and correct the false statements.

_____ **1** Some early records of Bill Gates were recently found.

_____ **2** The capacity to store a lot of digital records does not guarantee future access to them.

_____ **3** Maintaining access to out-of-date interactive applications is particularly difficult.

_____ **4** Google is working on this problem and will reveal their solution soon.

_____ **5** Satyanarayanan has been working on this problem but has not been able to solve it.

_____ **6** All government records are currently stored in the cloud.

READING BETWEEN THE LINES

7 MAKING INFERENCES **Work with a partner. Discuss the questions.**

1 In paragraph 1, the writer states, "the people who found these items would be very excited—at least at first." Why would they be excited?

2 Why does the writer make a comparison to the Dark Ages?

3 What do you think the term *bit rot* means? Think about the meaning of a *bit* in the digital world.

4 Why is it more difficult to preserve a conversation thread on Twitter than in a letter?

⌁ CRITICAL THINKING

8 **Work with a partner. Discuss the questions.**

UNDERSTAND	APPLY	EVALUATE
What is a *time capsule*? What is it used for?	Have you ever found a box of memorabilia? Describe the experience.	Do you think it is important to save records of everyday life? Why or why not?

⚇ COLLABORATION

9 **A** Work in a small group. Imagine that your school is putting up a new building and wants to place a time capsule in its walls. Make a list of five things that represent today's student life and school spirit to contribute to the time capsule.

B Present your list to the class, and explain your reasons for choosing each item.

C As a class, decide on five things to contribute to the time capsule.

PREPARING TO READ

1 UNDERSTANDING KEY VOCABULARY **Read the sentences and choose the best definition for each vocabulary item in bold.**

1 The store that was once here closed five years ago, and the building has been **vacant** ever since.

    a busy   **b** for sale   **c** empty

2 We are looking for an **affordable** apartment, but everywhere we look the rents are too high.

    a not expensive   **b** average   **c** small but comfortable

3 **Developers** are going to build a shopping mall just outside of the city.

    a construction companies

    b companies that make a profit from buying and selling land

    c companies that buy land and build on it

4 The old building is falling apart, so the **renovation** is going to be very complex and expensive.

    a the replacement of an old building with a new one

    b the repair of a building to bring it into good condition

    c investment of money in an old building

5 The athletic **facility** at the university has a new ice-skating rink.

    a a building for a special purpose

    b a field

    c a place where people can meet

6 The government **maintains** that it has no money to pay for any new social programs.

    a continues to claim   **b** finally understands   **c** deeply regrets

7 The patient's condition has **deteriorated** rapidly. Doctors are doing their best to save her.

    a grown worse   **b** stabilized   **c** strengthened

8 After a period of adjustment, most immigrants find jobs and **prosper** in their new country.

    a stay   **b** are successful   **c** are optimistic

2 USING YOUR KNOWLEDGE **Read the fact box and then answer the questions.**

Palace of the Governors

- **The most expensive renovation in history –** Experts disagree. Perhaps St. Paul's Cathedral in London (about $64 million dollars; completed 2011). Perhaps the Pentagon in Arlington, VA, USA ($700 million; completed 2011), but much of the work was not renovation but complete rebuilding of sections destroyed on September 11, 2001.

- **The oldest operating hospital in the United States –** The Pennsylvania Hospital, Philadelphia, PA; built 1751; most recent renovation—a new roof (still being installed)

- **The oldest operating public building in the United States –** Palace of the Governors, Santa Fe, New Mexico; built between 1601 and 1618

- **The average cost of remodeling a kitchen in the United States –** about $20,000

1 Why might experts disagree about the most expensive renovation in history? _____

_____

2 How was part of the Pentagon destroyed in 2001? _____

_____

3 What is the difference between renovating and remodeling? _____

_____

3 SKIMMING **Skim the texts on pages 24–26 and answer the questions.**

1 What kind of texts are these?

_____

_____

2 Who is the intended audience?

_____

_____

3 Who wrote them?

_____

_____

4 What do you think they will be about?

_____

_____

_____

BUILD IT UP OR TEAR IT DOWN?

Background

1 The Beck County Hospital building is a vacant structure at 1200 Patterson Street in Whitbeck, Illinois. It was formerly home to the largest medical facility in central Illinois. The building opened in 1916 and was notable for being the first North American hospital with a central air conditioning system. The building's architect, C. Peter Randolph, said he employed an ornate Beaux Arts façade to "acknowledge beauty in the face of infirmity and attest the dignity of those we serve." Influences on Randolph's design included the core structures of Chicago's Cook County Hospital. In 2002, at the peak of its operations, the Beck County Hospital had 380 beds and 279 attending physicians. Although numerous updates were made to the building over the years, the Beck County Board (trustees of the hospital) determined in 2005 that full modernization was no longer feasible[1]. In 2008, the hospital's operations moved to a new facility in nearby Woodcroft. The original building, owned by Beck County, has remained unused since then.

[1]**feasible** (adj) possible or reasonable to do

New Neighborhood Group

123 South Avenue
Suite 306
Whitbeck, IL 60201
312.555.5555
hello@newneighborhood.org
www.newneighborhood.org

Dear Members of the County Board:

2 Beck County Hospital (BCH), which has been standing **vacant** for more than ten years, has become an eyesore[2] in our neighborhood. In spite of the fact that the government has spent millions of dollars studying the best use for the site, we are still waiting for action. Let's stop trying to figure out how to save this out-of-date pile of bricks. Our neighborhood is expanding and **prospering**, and it's about time for the board to show some leadership by adopting a proposal that embraces the future, not one that clings to the past.

3 It has been argued that it would be cheaper to reuse the old building than to tear it down and build a new one. Almost ten years ago, experts estimated that saving the BCH building would cost more than 150 million dollars. This figure may have been true then, but over the last decade, the building has **deteriorated** considerably, which would no doubt add to the cost of any **renovation** carried out today. Our experts agree that updating this one hundred-year-old building to meet modern safety standards would actually be more expensive than starting from scratch[3].

4 What this neighborhood needs is an up-to-date, green structure that will provide much-needed housing and retail space. Our proposal will replace the decaying hospital building with a hotel, apartments (including 15% **affordable** housing), and space for stores, restaurants, and medical offices. Just as important, construction of these structures, and the businesses that will be located in them, will provide good jobs for people in the community. How much longer do we have to wait for our leaders to make the right decision for the future of our neighborhood? Tear down BCH!

Respectfully yours,

New Neighborhood Group

[2]**eyesore** (n) something ugly and unpleasant to look at
[3]**start from scratch** (v) start over from the very beginning

Citizens Neighborhood Coalition

Dear Beck County Board:

5 Beck County Hospital, which welcomed patients and their families for almost a century, is a community landmark. The building is beautiful, but more beautiful than the structure itself is the statement it made to the city and the world. When it opened its doors in 1916, Beck County Hospital offered an attractive, modern **facility**, not just to the city's elite, but also to the poor. It sent the message that the poor are just as deserving of quality healthcare as the wealthy. People in the neighborhood called the hospital, our Statue of Liberty. Let's make sure this site continues to serve all of our citizens by renovating it now.

6 Some opponents to our proposal have argued that renovation is too expensive, but a recent, similar project demonstrated that this may not be the case. In fact, renovating an existing structure can cost about $25 per square foot less than even the most basic new construction, while preserving the beauty of the original building. And, although it is often claimed that old buildings have a more significant environmental footprint[4] compared with new construction, architect and sustainability expert Carl Elefante **maintains** that the greenest building is the one that is already built. New construction almost always has a more serious environmental impact because it requires the use of all new materials.

7 Our group's proposal for renovation of the hospital site and building will allow it to continue to serve the community by providing affordable housing, medical clinics, a school, and a community center—resources that we badly need. If instead we allow **developers** to take over the project, the guiding principle will be profit, not neighborhood preservation. The people who will benefit most will be the investors in the project, not the people of our community. Save the Beck County Hospital building!

Respectfully,
Citizens Neighborhood Coalition

123 North Avenue, Suite 1275 | Whitbeck, IL 60201 | 312.555.5555 | www.cncil.org

[4]**environmental footprint** (n) the impact something/someone has on the environment

WHILE READING

4 READING FOR MAIN IDEAS **Read the texts on pages 24–26. Then complete the tasks.**

1   Which group makes the argument that the hospital should be torn down?

_____

2   Underline or highlight a sentence in the letter that expresses this argument.

3   Which group makes the argument that the hospital should be renovated?

_____

4   Underline or highlight a sentence in the letter that expresses this argument.

✎ SKILLS

IDENTIFYING SUPPORTING DETAILS

Writers support their arguments with details, such as reasons, explanations, or examples.

5 READING FOR DETAILS **Read the texts again. Then complete the tasks.**

1   What reasons does the New Neighborhood Group give to support its argument?
     Its proposal …

   a   is cheaper.

   b   has more community support.

   c   can be completed more quickly.

   d   will provide jobs.

   e   will last longer.

2   Underline or highlight these reasons in the letter.

3   What reasons does the Citizens Neighborhood Coalition give to support its argument?
     Its proposal …

   a   is cheaper.

   b   meets more of the community's needs.

   c   is more popular with the community.

   d   is more practical.

   e   is greener.

4   Underline or highlight these reasons in the letter.

READING BETWEEN THE LINES

6 IDENTIFYING PURPOSE **Work with a partner. Discuss the questions.**

1   What is the purpose of paragraph 1?

2   Who do you think are the people behind the New Neighborhood Group? What are the group's goals generally?

3   Who do you think are the people behind the Citizens Neighborhood Coalition? What are this group's goals generally?

4   Why do you think Beck County Hospital was once compared to the Statue of Liberty?

5   What does the statement "the greenest building is the one that is already built" mean?

☼ CRITICAL THINKING

7 SYNTHESIZING **Work with a partner. Use ideas from Reading 1 and Reading 2 to discuss the questions.**

APPLY	APPLY	EVALUATE
What is *gentrification*? Think of three benefits and three drawbacks.	Apart from the thing itself, what do you think is lost when something from the past disappears?	Do you think it is better to try to preserve old buildings or tear them down to make way for new ones, even if the buildings are beautiful or historically important? Explain.

🖧 COLLABORATION

8 **Work in a small group. Prepare a role play. Practice with your group. Then perform it for the class.**

Situation:

Property developers want to gentrify an old neighborhood in your town. The neighborhood is not fancy. Some buildings need a lot of repair, but the people who live and work there like their community.

Roles and positions:

- The manager of a city's planning department - You have the power to approve or deny development permits necessary to for anyone to make big changes to a neighborhood.
- A property developer - You believe that gentrification is a good thing. You do not live in the neighborhood.
- The owner of a small business in the neighborhood - You live in the neighborhood, and you do not want the area to be gentrified.
- A home owner in the neighborhood - You love your community but are thinking about selling your home and retiring in the Florida Keys. You have mixed feelings about gentrification.

Role play:

You are all at a meeting at the planning department's offices. The purpose is to determine if permits will be given to the property developer. The manager directs the meeting. All sides present their opinions, and ask and answer questions. At the end, the manager makes the final decision.

TIME EXPRESSIONS

LANGUAGE

There are many different phrases that can tell the reader when or how something happens. There are also phrases that describe things and events as they relate to a stated or implied timeframe.

when	how	in relation to a timeframe
at the turn of the century over the past / last + (week / month / year) at one time for the time being	slowly but surely in a flash in the blink of an eye	up to date out of date it's about time for

1 Complete the sentences with an appropriate expression. In some items, more than one answer is possible.

1 The clothes she wears are really _____. People have not worn jackets like that since the 1980s.

2 _____ you to find a job. I am not going to support you any longer.

3 After a two-year downturn, _____ the economy is showing signs of recovery.

4 Twenty years ago, _____, Twitter, Instagram, and Snapchat did not yet exist.

5 _____ this was the most popular restaurant in the city. Today, however, it's hardly ever full, even on Saturday nights.

6 I called the police and they got here _____ . I was surprised by how quickly they arrived.

7 If my company keeps doing well, we should be able to buy a house in the next couple of years, but _____, we're renting an apartment.

8 _____ five years, the city has torn down more than ten historic buildings.

9 The owners have kept the building _____ with new lighting and an efficient heating system.

2 On your own or with a partner, complete the sentences with your own ideas using time expressions.

1 For the time being, I'm _____

_____

2 Slowly but surely, the world / country / city _____

_____

3 In order to stay up to date with technology, I _____

_____

4 In the blink of an eye, _____

_____

5 It's about time for me _____

_____

6 At one time, this _____

_____

COMPOUND ADJECTIVES

LANGUAGE

An adjective can be a single word or a phrase of two or more words acting as a single modifier. Depending on the type of phrase and its position in the sentence, the words may need to be hyphenated.

Before a noun, a compound adjective should be hyphenated.

We need more **up-to-date** reference materials.

My company just installed **state-of-the-art** graphics programs on all our computers.

When the same phrase appears in other contexts, no hyphenation is necessary.

I try to keep my software **up to date**.

This program was **state of the art** about ten years ago!

The gentrified Wynwood Arts District in Miami, Florida

3 **Circle the correct option to complete the sentences.**

1   We need a more *long term* / *long-term* solution to this problem.

2   This city needs housing for *low income* / *low-income* families.

3   These homes were built at the *turn of the century* / *turn-of-the-century*, but they already need a lot of repair.

4   The neighborhood has implemented a system of *one way* / *one-way* streets to ease the increasing volume of traffic.

5   The artists in this area are quite *well known* / *well-known*.

6   Where there once were apartments, today most of the buildings are *single family* / *single-family* homes.

7   Appliances installed in newly constructed homes must meet strict government standards and also be *energy efficient* / *energy-efficient*.

8   As in any *fast growing* / *fast-growing* community, we face a number of challenges.

4 **Write five sentences using a compound adjective from the first column and an appropriate noun from the second column. Compare sentences with a partner. Did you choose the same word sets?**

compound adjectives	nouns
low-income	homes / windows / light bulb
well-known	neighborhood / housing / apartments
long-term	author / song / story
energy-efficient	industry / city / business
fast-growing	goal / plan / care

1   _____

_____

2   _____

_____

3   _____

_____

4   _____

_____

5   _____

_____

WATCH AND LISTEN

PREPARING TO WATCH

1 ACTIVATING YOUR KNOWLEDGE **Work with a partner. Discuss the questions.**

1 Do you own a collection of music or movies? Is it stored on discs in your home or in a digital download folder on your computer?

2 Do you still have any CDs or DVDs? How long do you think they will last?

3 What could you do to preserve your CDs and DVDs? What other belongings do you have that might need to be preserved?

2 PREDICTING CONTENT USING VISUALS **Look at the pictures from the video. Discuss the questions with your partner.**

1 What problem do you think the woman is investigating?

2 Why do you think it is a problem?

3 What do you think will be learned by the research the woman is doing?

WHILE WATCHING

3 UNDERSTANDING MAIN IDEAS **Watch the video. Which sentence best expresses the main idea of the video?**

a The Library of Congress is testing the longevity of CDs every three to five years. ☐

b CDs are being aged to help learn which type of manufacturing is best for CD development. ☐

c How a CD is manufactured, how it has been handled, and how it has been stored all affect its longevity. ☐

4 UNDERSTANDING DETAILS **Watch the video again. Write a detail for each main idea.**

1   Fanella France and her colleagues are studying the preservation of CDs.

_____

2   To test CD durability, the Library of Congress is accelerating aging.

_____

3   There are several things people can do to preserve their CDs at home.

_____

5 MAKING INFERENCES **Work with a partner. Discuss the questions.**

1   Why is it important for the Library of Congress to understand CD preservation?

2   What other items might the Preservation Research and Testing department of the Library of Congress be researching and testing?

3   What kinds of conditions might negatively affect old books, CDs, films, etc.? How might they go about testing these items under different conditions?

☼ CRITICAL THINKING

6 **Work with a partner. Discuss the questions.**

APPLY	ANALYZE	EVALUATE
What are some other items that are usually preserved in national libraries or museums?	Can we really learn from the past, or do we learn just as much when we focus on the present and the future?	Is there value in preserving technology, media, or buildings in their original format? Explain your reasons.

⚙ COLLABORATION

7 **A** Work in a small group to make an infographic. Do research. Identify three countries or regions where important art, buildings, or records were destroyed in the past or are threatened today.

B On a large sheet of paper or poster, draw an outline of the continents of the world. Put a dot in each country or region that you identified in step A. Near each dot, make a fact box with the following information:

- Name of the country
- What was/is threatened?
- Who threatened/threatens it?
- Why?
- The results

C Add visuals of the threatened objects, and share your infographic with the class.

DESIGN

LEARNING OBJECTIVES

Key Reading Skills	Making inferences; using an outline to take notes
Additional Reading Skills	Using your knowledge; understanding key vocabulary; previewing; reading for main ideas; taking notes; identifying purpose; reading for details; synthesizing
Language Development	Describing emotional responses; paraphrasing

ACTIVATE YOUR KNOWLEDGE

Work with a partner. Discuss the questions.

1   How many different brands of shoes are in this photo? Can you tell? Why or why not?

2   If you had to pick one pair of these shoes for yourself, which would you pick? Why would you pick that one over the others?

3   If the shoes all had a familiar logo, would it be easier to choose? What does a logo tell you about the product it is on?

READING 1

1 USING YOUR KNOWLEDGE Find photos of a professional golfer and a professional race car and/or driver. Company logos should be visible on the clothes and equipment in the photos. Write the logos you recognize in the correct column in the chart. Compare lists with a partner. Discuss which logos are the most effective and why.

GOLFER	RACE CAR

2 UNDERSTANDING KEY VOCABULARY **Read the sentences and write the words in bold next to the definitions.**

1 The judges used specific **criteria** to rate the performance of the athletes.

2 The initial report said that the business had made a 10% profit last year, but a **subsequent** report corrected the amount to 7%.

3 There are just a few news stories in the magazine; most of it is **devoted to** advertising.

4 My husband likes traditional art and furniture, but I prefer a more **contemporary** style.

5 The movie is quite violent, so it is not **appropriate** for young children.

6 Access to food and safe drinking water are both basic **human rights**.

7 The Red Cross is asking for **donations** of food and clothing to help victims of the earthquake.

8 The best way to **retain** good employees is to pay them a good salary.

a _____ (adj) existing or happening now

b _____ (n) fair and moral treatment that every person deserves

c _____ (adj) next; happening after something else

d _____ (n) money or goods given in order to help people

e _____ (n pl) standards used for judging something

f _____ (v) to keep; to continue having

g _____ (adj) correct or right for a particular situation

h _____ (adj) for one particular purpose

3 PREVIEWING **You are going to read a chapter from a marketing textbook about logos. Work with a partner. Preview the text and discuss these questions.**

1 How would you answer the title question?

2 Would you say all of the logos in the text are successful? Why or why not?

CHAPTER 5

WHAT MAKES A SUCCESSFUL LOGO?

1 In 2010, a group of world leaders got together to bring greater attention to **human rights**. They held a design competition for a logo that any organization **devoted to** human rights issues could use.

2 A logo is an efficient visual form that conveys an organization's message. Logos may seem rather simple. After all, they are often just a name or very basic image, but in fact, designing a good logo takes a lot of time and thought. So, what were the world leaders looking for? What are the **criteria** that define a good logo? If you ask ten different graphic designers, you may get ten different answers. However, there are some common themes.

3 A good logo is clear and simple. Simple logos are easy to remember. In studies where participants were shown hundreds of unfamiliar logos, the ones they remembered later all had simple designs. Some designers advise the use of no more than two colors.

4 A good logo must also be unique so it won't be confused with the logo from another organization. For example, the logo for IKEA is so familiar that any new logo in those shades of blue and yellow would probably remind people of IKEA. A unique logo also arouses curiosity when people see it for the first time. They want to know more about it. When tennis star Novak Djokovic began wearing shirts by the Japanese clothing manufacturer UNIQLO, people unfamiliar with the company became curious about the odd combination of letters that make up its logo.

¹**retro** (adj) having the appearance of something from the past
²**nonprofit** (adj) established for a reason other than making a profit, often for the arts or for religious or charitable purposes

5 Logos should be flexible enough to adapt across time and placement. We all remember Apple's rainbow-colored design, which worked in the 1970s, but today would look retro[1]. The **subsequent** gray and black Apple logo looks more **contemporary**, yet it **retains** the original design. Designers also need to consider where the logo will appear. Will it be on shopping bags? Coffee cups? Does it need to shrink down to a tiny icon on a digital device, like the Twitter bluebird or the Facebook *f*? Will people be able to recognize it from far away on the side of a truck?

6 More than anything else, a logo needs to tell a story—to convey the company's identity and evoke an emotional response in the people who see it. But to be successful, the message and the response must be **appropriate** for the organization that the logo represents. The Toys R Us logo, with its childish handwriting and backwards *R*, conveys a message of fun. It is childlike and playful. It works for a toy company, but it probably would not work for a bank or insurance company.

7 In contrast, the FedEx logo, with the negative space in its block letters forming a forward-pointing arrow, looks like serious business. Its aim is to inspire confidence: We are a company you can trust your package to. An emotional response is particularly important for nonprofit[2] organizations. The World Wide Fund for Nature (WWF) hopes that its iconic black and white panda will resonate with the public and encourage people to make a **donation** to support its global environmental conservation work on saving the endangered species and their habitats as well as reducing people's footprint for a sustainable future.

8 Once a logo becomes widely recognized, businesses and organizations often rely more on the logo than their name. The public immediately recognizes the Nike swoosh, McDonald's golden arches, and Target's red and white circles because these logos have become so familiar.

9 So, what logo did world leaders hope would convey an immediately recognizable and unmistakable message of human rights? They chose Serbian designer Predrag Stakić's logo, which combines the images of a bird and a human hand.

PROTECTING LOGOS

A business can protect its brand name and its logo by getting them trademarked. In the United States, this protection is granted by a federal agency, the Department of Commerce. After you register your trademark, no one can use your name or logo without permission. This is meant to keep your valuable mark off fake goods. It also prohibits the trademark's use in ways that might damage your company's image.

4 READING FOR MAIN IDEAS **Read the textbook chapter. Then check (✓) the statement that gives the most complete and accurate description of a good logo.**

a   A good logo is easy for anybody to recognize and understand.   ☐

b   A good logo expresses a company's identity in a way that is
easy to recognize.   ☐

c   A good logo will last forever in the public's mind.   ☐

d   A good logo helps the company to make a profit.   ☐

5 TAKING NOTES **Complete the outline with information from Reading 1. Fill in main ideas, details, and examples. Where the outline has extra spaces for examples, add some of your own.**

Criteria for a successful logo

I.   Efficient form of visual communication
   A. simple and easy to remember
   B. _____ so won't be confused with other logos.
      1. Example: _____
      2. _____
   C. arouse _____
      1. Example: _____
      2. Example: _____

II.   _____ and adaptable
   A. across _____
      1. Example: _____
      2. Example: _____
   B. _____
      1. can shrink
         Example: _____
      2. _____
         Example: _____

III.   _____
   A. _____
      Example: _____
   B. _____
      Example: _____

READING BETWEEN THE LINES

🔧 SKILLS

MAKING INFERENCES

Writers often suggest ideas but do not say them directly. In this case, readers need to *infer* what the writer means. Inferring meaning is an important reading skill. Readers combine what the writer says with logic and their own knowledge of the world to infer the complete meaning of the text.

6 MAKING INFERENCES **Work with a partner. Go online and look at the UNIQLO logo. What about its design aroused so much curiosity, do you think? Write down some ideas.**

_____

_____

7 IDENTIFYING PURPOSE **Think of three nonprofit organizations of different types and look up their logos. What kind of responses do you think they want to evoke with their logos? Are they successful?**

nonprofit	response
1 _____	_____
2 _____	_____
3 _____	_____

💡 CRITICAL THINKING

8 **Work in small groups. Discuss the questions.**

APPLY

Choose one of the logos discussed in Reading 1. What story do you think it is meant to tell?

ANALYZE

Think of another logo that you think is not as successful as those in Reading 1. Describe and analyze its effectiveness.

EVALUATE

Is the human rights logo successful based on the criteria discussed in Reading 1? Why or why not?

👥 COLLABORATION

9 **A** Work in a small group. Imagine that you work for Maple State Bank and that you must create a new logo. Your bank serves ordinary families and small businesses in your city. Design a logo that will relate to your customers and community.

B Present and promote your logo to the class.

C As a class, vote on the best logo and story.

SOCIAL MEDIA AHEAD

READING 2

1 USING YOUR KNOWLEDGE **You are going to read a chapter about rebranding and logos. Look at the table on page 46. Discuss the questions with a partner.**

1 Have you ever bought products by the manufacturers on the list of frequently faked products? Were you concerned that your purchase was a fake?

2 Why do you think the number of fake BIC products is so large?

3 What types of products are the most commonly faked? Why?

4 How might statistics of fake branded items relate to a reading about rebranding and logos?

2 UNDERSTANDING KEY VOCABULARY **Read the sentences and choose the best definition for each vocabulary item in bold.**

1 There has been tremendous **opposition to** the new law requiring voters to show a photo identification card.

   a doubts about

   b disagreement with

   c misunderstandings about

2 The two sisters **resemble** each other so much that many people think they are twins.

   a look like

   b sound like

   c compete with

3 This clothing brand is designed to **appeal to** teenage girls and young women.

   a send a message to

   b sell to

   c be interesting or attractive to

4 For a long time, the community **resisted** the proposal to close our school, but we finally had to accept it.

   a tried to change

   b ignored

   c fought against

5 For a long time, the government has **modified** its policy so that more people can apply for financial aid for college.

   a changed somewhat

   b renewed

   c started

6   Because I am trying to lose weight, I usually **opt for** water instead of soft drinks or juice.

   a   refuse

   b   choose

   c   prefer

7   Many people **associate** specific foods with experiences in their childhood.

   a   remember in a positive way

   b   continue thinking about

   c   make a connection in one's mind with

8   His role in the company has **evolved** over the past ten years. He began as a salesperson, but now he works with clients to build new products just for their needs.

   a   become less useful

   b   developed slowly

   c   stayed the same

3 PREVIEWING **Preview the reading on pages 44–46. Discuss the questions with a partner.**

1   The chapter title uses the word *brand* to describe an action and adds the prefix *re-*. What do you think the process of *rebranding* involves?

2   Look at the images in this chapter. What role do you think logos might play in the rebranding process?

3   What are some of your favorite brands of casual clothing and shoes? How do their logos and advertising relate to their company image?

CHAPTER 6
REBRANDING AND LOGOS

1 Businesses need to be able to change as markets change. To keep up with changes, they frequently update their brands and advertising in a process called *rebranding*. Rebranding often prompts these companies to redesign their logos at the same time. Take, for example, NBC (the National Broadcasting Company). This company started in the days of radio, thus the microphone in its original logo from 1944. As it moved into television and then color television, the company adopted its iconic peacock design in 1956. Since then, it has updated "the Bird" several times to reflect the tastes and styles of the times.

2 Rebranding and new logo designs may be needed because a company has changed its focus. For example, Xerox, a company whose primary product was once photocopiers, wanted to call attention to the fact that it handles a much wider range of document technology now. Some companies may want to change their image because there have been some negative associations with their old one. For example, the logo for oil company British Petroleum (BP) looked like any sign you might see at a gas station. Customers often **associate** gasoline with climate change and a negative impact on the environment, so BP **opted for** a "greener" logo, one that **resembles** a sunflower. Kentucky Fried Chicken wanted to distance itself from unhealthy fried foods. When it redesigned the product's logo, the word "fried" disappeared and only the initials KFC remained.

3   Some brands simply mature and need a new logo to show this. Many hi-tech companies, often founded by young entrepreneurs, begin with logos that reflect the age of their founders. If the companies are successful and begin to **appeal to** a wider audience, they may want to **modify** their logo. Both Spotify and Snapchat have gone through this process. Spotify's earlier, youthful logo has recently **evolved** into a simple graphic that evokes sound waves. Snapchat's cute ghost has lost its silly face, retaining only the figure's outline.

4   The public generally **resists** changes to familiar logos at first. However, **opposition to** the new design usually dies down after a while, especially if the new logo retains some familiar elements. For example, the new BP logo kept the color scheme of the old logo, and the new KFC logo retains the brand's familiar bearded face of its founder, Colonel Sanders. If there is too much change, however, customers may become confused or reject the change. Executives at PepsiCo found this out when they changed the logo for one of their brands: Tropicana orange juice. Customers were looking for the familiar orange with a straw; they did not recognize the product with the new logo as Tropicana. Sales dropped dramatically, and Tropicana brought back the old logo.

5   A final reason for a new logo design comes from technology. New platforms[1] may necessitate modifications. As devices become smaller, logos need to be simpler and easier to recognize on a small scale. Companies like Airbnb and PayPal dropped their names and chose simpler graphics for their latest logos so that users can identify them more easily on their mobile devices.

▌[1]**platform** (n) the type of system a computer or smartphone uses

6 Changes in technology can place limits on logo designs, but they can also offer new options. In particular, as more business and personal interactions take place in digital environments, more companies are creating logos that are animated and interactive. The foremost example of this is Google's new logo, which appeared in 2015. The new logo has the same four basic colors as the old logo, but it transforms into a number of different images, depending on the product. For example, at the start of a Google voice search, the logo transforms into four dots in the Google colors, then into four wiggling lines that look like sound waves.

7 New logos can be expensive. The sunflower logo cost BP close to $200 million, and Tropicana lost $33 million on its new logo. Yet, for most companies, the process can inject new energy into a brand and is therefore considered worth the investment.

Figure 1 Fake Branded Items Seized by Customs Officials Worldwide, 2014

Brand	Items seized
BIC (pens, lighters, etc.)	3,809,000
FIFA (soccer merchandise)	2,261,110
Elite (cameras, clothing, etc.)	1,630.000
Michael Kors (watches, wallets, etc.)	1,321,387
Walt Disney (character-related merchandise)	1, 261,977
Adidas (sports shoes and equipment)	1,226,488
Angry Birds (character-related merchandise)	1,201,320

Source: World Customs Organization, Nov 2015

WHILE READING

4 READING FOR MAIN IDEAS **Read the excerpt on pages 44–46. Then check (✓) all the circumstances mentioned in the reading that might prompt a company to redesign its logo.**

a   The company wants to appeal to younger consumers.   ☐

b   Changes in technology require it.   ☐

c   The public does not like the old logo.   ☐

d   The company wants the public to forget about something negative.   ☐

5 READING FOR DETAILS **Match the reasons for a logo redesign to the company.**

1   need to fit logo on mobile devices   a   British Petroleum

2   company and founders have matured   b   Google

3   wider range of products   c   Snapchat

4   opportunities provided by new technology   d   Xerox

5   negative associations   e   NBC

6   need to refresh look over time   f   PayPal

Using an outline to take notes on a reading can help deepen your understanding of the reading and help you remember more of the details. Main ideas provide the basic organization for an outline, with supporting details listed underneath them.

Outlines do not always need to be formal, like the one on page 40, with numbers, letters, and single words. You can use a less formal organization to take more extensive, but less formal, notes.

6 TAKING NOTES **Read the article again. Take notes using the informal structure below. Compare your notes with a partner.**

I.   Change in focus

_____

_____

_____

II. Brand has matured

_____

_____

_____

III. Problems with rebranding

_____

_____

_____

IV. Impact of changing technology

_____

_____

_____

READING BETWEEN THE LINES

7 MAKING INFERENCES **Work with a partner. Choose the statement(s) that can you infer from Reading 2. Discuss your reasoning.**

a   A peacock is immediately associated with the idea of color.   ☐

b   The founders of Spotify were young when they started the company.   ☐

c   The new BP logo was a success.   ☐

d   The face on KFC's logo is an important element of the brand.   ☐

e   Other companies now have animated logos like Google's.   ☐

⌖ CRITICAL THINKING

8 SYNTHESIZING **Work with a partner. Use ideas from Reading 1 and Reading 2 to discuss the questions.**

APPLY	ANALYZE	EVALUATE
Describe your response to a specific logo, and compare it to your partner's.	Choose one of the pairs of logos discussed in Reading 2. Why do you think the company made the change?	How important do you think a logo is for a brand? Support your idea with examples.

🗇 COLLABORATION

9 A   Work in a small group. Brainstorm a list of at least three logos that you think are not attractive or effective. Take notes on your discussion.

B   Choose one of the logos to improve. Decide on some changes that would make the logo better.

C   Re-design your logo on a poster board or computer. Present "before" and "after" versions of the logo to the class, and explain your changes.

DESCRIBING EMOTIONAL RESPONSES

1 Study the table of common verb + noun collocations used to describe emotional responses. Do these expressions describe positive, negative, or mixed responses?

verbs	nouns	response
evoke	feeling(s), memories, emotions	a *mixed*
inspire	confidence, awe, fear	b
arouse	interest, curiosity, suspicion, anger	c
stir up	trouble, opposition, feelings, anger	d
generate	interest, excitement, enthusiasm	e
provoke	response, controversy, outrage, anger, anxiety	f

2 Complete the sentences with an appropriate collocation. In some items, more than one answer is possible.

1 The man wore a hat pulled down over his eyes and a large coat that seemed to be covering something. His appearance immediately _____.

2 The new law that requires non-citizens to carry a special identity card at all times has _____ .

3 The new line of computer products and accessories has _____ a lot of _____ among tech-savvy buyers.

4 With his strong positions and years of experience, the presidential candidate _____ among voters.

5 The insults against the rap singer _____ an angry _____ from his many fans.

6 Songs from the past often _____ happy _____.

3 Write three sentences of your own using some of the collocations in the table in Exercise 1 to describe emotional responses.

1 _____

_____

2 _____

_____

3 _____

_____

PARAPHRASING

LANGUAGE

When you paraphrase, you put another person's ideas into your own words. Use synonyms and different grammatical structures to express the ideas in a new form without changing their meaning. You may also need to arrange the ideas in a different order.

Changes in technology can place limits on **logo designs,** but **they can also offer new options.**

At the same time that emerging technology restricts **logo designs, it can also open up new possibilities.**

If you use identifiable phrasing from the original text, you must use quotation marks.

4 Paraphrase the sentences.

1 Logos are symbols commonly used by companies and other organizations to promote their identity and to increase public recognition.

2 Many companies choose logos that reflect their names, origins, or products so that consumers can easily associate the logo with the company.

3 Color is a crucial element of any logo because colors help anchor the logo in consumers' memories, allowing them to distinguish the logo from other, similar logos.

4 Logos of sports teams, found on clothing, souvenirs, and other merchandising products, are a major source of revenue for teams.

5 Paraphrase two sentences from Reading 1 that describe the criteria for a successful logo.

1

2

GLOSSARY

endemic (adj)   found particularly in a specific area or group

zany (adj)   surprisingly different and strange, and therefore amusing and interesting

typography (n)   the design of writing in a piece of printing or on a computer screen

Helvetica (n)   a typeface or font that has clean, smooth lines

in full swing (adv)   at the height of an activity

authoritarian (adj)   demanding total obedience to one's authority

PREPARING TO WATCH

1 ACTIVATING YOUR KNOWLEDGE   **Work with a partner. Discuss the questions.**

1   How have ads changed in your lifetime?

2   What companies spend the most on advertising?

3   What are some subtle ways that companies try to influence what you buy?

2 PREDICTING CONTENT USING VISUALS   **Look at the pictures from the video. Discuss the questions with your partner.**

1   Which ads do you think are more effective? Why?

2   How does the look of the letters—the font—differ in each picture?

3   How do you think the font affects the look of a logo, ad, or sign?

4   Do you think the font affects the way people perceive the information? If so, how big a difference does it make?

5   What are the benefits of simple lettering?

WHILE WATCHING

3 UNDERSTANDING MAIN IDEAS   **Watch the video. Which sentence best expresses the main idea of the video?**

a   The ad for Coca-Cola is the most effective ad ever.   ☐

b   Many corporations today use Helvetica because it communicates a clear message.   ☐

c   Companies like to use Helvetica today so they appear strong and authoritarian.   ☐

4 UNDERSTANDING DETAILS **Watch the video again. Write examples for each main idea.**

1   In the 1950s, bad typography was prevalent.

_____

_____

2   Helvetica has several characteristics that make it successful.

_____

_____

5 MAKING INFERENCES **Work with a partner. Discuss the questions.**

1   Why do you think there was a wide variety of lettering designs in the 1950s?

2   How do you think the man feels about the use of exclamation points? How do you know?

3   Why do you think a corporation or government wants to appear accessible? How might that benefit consumers and citizens?

⚙ CRITICAL THINKING

6 **Discuss the questions with your partner.**

APPLY	APPLY	EVALUATE
Describe an ad or sign that you find very attractive. Why do you think it appeals to you?	Describe an ad or sign that you find difficult to read or unpleasant to look at. What is the problem with it?	Which type of lettering do you prefer, the typography in the ads from the 1950s, or the ones of today? Why?

🗣 COLLABORATION

7 **A** Work in a small group. Skim at least five print or digital ads. Choose a font (other than Helvetica) that is used in one or more of them.

   B Find the following information about the font:

   • its name
   • who designed it
   • when it was designed
   • its original use
   • its advantages
   • its disadvantages
   • your response to it

   C Organize a short group presentation, and present your findings to the class.

PRIVACY

LEARNING OBJECTIVES

Key Reading Skills	Previewing; identifying purpose and tone
Additional Reading Skills	Understanding key vocabulary; using your knowledge; reading for main ideas; reading for details; taking notes; annotating; synthesizing
Language Development	Collocations for behavior; problem-solution collocations

ACTIVATE YOUR KNOWLEDGE

Work with a partner. Discuss the questions.

1 How much time do you spend on the Internet every day? What sites do you spend the most time on?

2 In what ways do you interact publicly on the Internet other than social media? For example, do you post videos or comment on others' videos, comment on articles, review restaurants?

3 Do you know everyone you interact with online? How easy is it to communicate with total strangers?

PREPARING TO READ

1 UNDERSTANDING KEY VOCABULARY **Read the sentences and write the words in bold next to the definitions.**

1 We **guarantee** that you will not find a cheaper price for this computer anywhere.

2 She felt deep anger and **humiliation** when she learned that her private emails and photos had been published on the Internet.

3 The children had experienced years of **abusive** physical and emotional treatment.

4 Several athletes had to **withdraw** from the game because of injuries.

5 She was in the hospital, so no one could doubt the **validity** of her excuse for missing the deadline.

6 She is extremely upset at the moment because she has just heard some very **disturbing** news.

7 The journalist claims that he received the information from an **anonymous** source. The person would not give his or her name.

8 This action was not only unacceptable, it also **violated** his basic human rights.

a _____ (adj) bad and cruel; causing another person mental or physical harm

b _____ (adj) upsetting; causing worry

c _____ (v) to promise absolutely or legally

d _____ (n) reasonableness or acceptability

e _____ (adj) unidentified or unidentifiable

f _____ (v) to break, such as a law or agreement

g _____ (n) shame and loss of self-respect

h _____ (v) to stop participating

2 USING YOUR KNOWLEDGE **You are going to read an article about cyber harassment. Work with a partner to complete the tasks.**

1 Use a dictionary to find the meaning of each part of the term.

cyber: _____

harassment: _____

2 Now explain to your partner what you think *cyber harassment* means.

🔧 SKILLS

PREVIEWING

It is useful to know something about the topic before you begin reading. Quickly reading the first sentence of each paragraph can give you a good idea of what the article will be about.

3 PREVIEWING **Preview the article on pages 58–59 by reading the first sentence of each paragraph. Check (✓) the topics you think will be discussed in the article. Compare answers with a partner. After you finish reading, come back to check your predictions.**

a   a comparison between online and face-to-face harassment   ☐

b   reasons why cyber harassment continues to occur   ☐

c   a description of cyber harassment   ☐

d   how victims can fight against people who harass them   ☐

e   a description of people who engage in cyber harassment   ☐

f   an explanation of the legal issues in cyber harassment   ☐

CYBER HARASSMENT

1 Bloggers like Amanda Hess know about it. Journalist Caroline Criado-Perez is also familiar with it. Online gamer Jenny Haniver knows it all too well. They all know about cyber harassment because they have all been victims. Cyber harassment ranges from behavior such as name calling online to more **disturbing** behavior, including threats of violence, posting embarrassing photos, and spreading personal or false information online. In the most serious cases, as in those of Hess, Criado-Perez, and Haniver, the harassment continues over a long period of time, with numerous offensive and threatening posts every day.

Journalist Caroline
Criado-Perez

2 A 2014 survey revealed that this kind of harassment is quite common. Almost three-quarters of all Internet users have seen it happen, and 40% have experienced it personally. It has been suggested that even these figures may not reflect the full extent of the problem. Cyber harassment is particularly common among younger Internet users, and women are more likely to experience its more serious forms. Criado-Perez made the suggestion online that the Bank of England should put more women on their banknotes. For this idea, she received hundreds of hostile comments against her personally and against women more generally. Haniver was the victim of ongoing **abusive** comments and threats for apparently no other reason than she was an assertive female gamer. Blogger Hess received similar treatment. You can easily find examples of cyber harassment on social media, in the comments section of many blogs and websites, and especially, in the online gaming world.

Trolls and Victims

3 Who is saying and doing all of these nasty things and why? The worst behavior is believed to come from so-called *trolls*, Internet users who disrupt Internet communication with negative and offensive actions and comments. These individuals take pleasure in insulting other users, causing them **humiliation** and pain. Studies suggest that some of these people have mental or emotional problems; however, experts believe that many people who engage in online abuse are otherwise unremarkable people. Harassing others simply brings them the attention and excitement that their lives in the offline world may lack. The cover of the Internet allows them, and perhaps even encourages them, to behave in ways that they never would in face-to-face situations.

4 Victims of this kind of harassment often ask why trolls are allowed to remain **anonymous**. Shouldn't people who are abusing the system be made to answer for their conduct? Victims also wonder why someone—the government, Internet service providers, or the social networking sites themselves (e.g., Facebook, Twitter, etc.)—does not do more to stop such attacks. Although these points have **validity**, eliminating anonymity and limiting what people can say on the Internet present problems of their own. Many people prefer not to reveal their identity online, not because they are trolls, but because they want to protect their own privacy. For example, you may want to ask questions in a chat room about a health problem that you do not want others to know about. Furthermore, limiting what people can say online or anywhere else could set a dangerous precedent. It could be seen as **violating** the constitutional right to free speech which **guarantees** all people the right to say what they want, even if it is unpopular or offensive.

A Real Threat

5 Because the harassment takes place online, it is not always taken seriously. A threat online may not seem as real as a threat that occurs face to face. Victims are often told not to be "drama queens." Yet, the impact of this harassment on its victims is very real and very damaging. They often suffer serious psychological shock and pain. They may lose their confidence and **withdraw** from all interaction on the Internet because they fear that they or their families will suffer abusive treatment in return. Recovery can be difficult, and for some, it never comes. For others, the experience prompts them to speak out. Jenny Haniver blogs, tweets, and speaks about her experiences of harassment in the world of gaming in hopes of bringing more public attention to this issue.

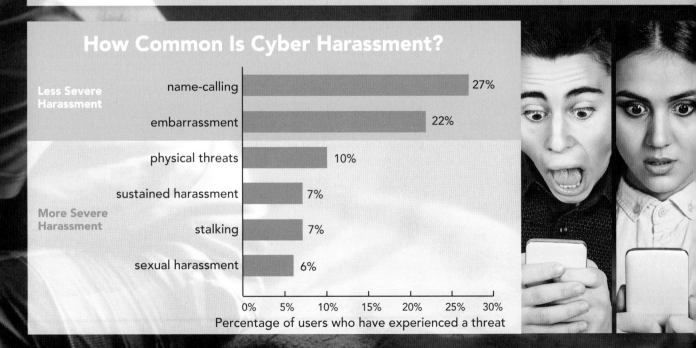

How Common Is Cyber Harassment?

Less Severe Harassment
- name-calling: 27%
- embarrassment: 22%

More Severe Harassment
- physical threats: 10%
- sustained harassment: 7%
- stalking: 7%
- sexual harassment: 6%

Percentage of users who have experienced a threat

WHILE READING

4 READING FOR MAIN IDEAS AND DETAILS **Read the article on pages 58–59. Then read these statements and write *MI* (main idea) or *SD* (supporting detail). Which paragraph does each one apply to?**

Statements	MI or SD	Paragraph
1 Complaints about cyber harassment by victims are sometimes considered too dramatic.	____	____
2 Trolls engage in disruptive behavior for a variety of reasons.	____	____
3 Forty percent of Internet users have experienced some form of cyber harassment.	____	____
4 It is difficult to stop cyber harassment.	____	____
5 Victims of cyber harassment often do not get a lot of support.	____	____
6 Cyber harassment takes many forms.	____	____
7 Limiting offensive speech may be considered a violation of the right to free speech.	____	____
8 Many Internet users experience cyber harassment.	____	____
9 Cyber harassment includes physical threats.	____	____
10 Trolls harass other Internet users because they enjoy causing pain.	____	____

5 TAKING NOTES **In your notebook, use your work in Exercise 4 to create an outline of the article. Look back at Unit 2 for help.**

READING BETWEEN THE LINES

🔧 SKILLS

IDENTIFYING PURPOSE AND TONE

Understanding the writer's purpose and his or her perspective on the topic can deepen your understanding of the material. Negative and positive words can help you determine if the writer is offering praise or criticism.

6 IDENTIFYING PURPOSE AND TONE **Work with a partner to complete the tasks.**

1 Choose the idea that best describes the writer's main purpose in writing this article.

    a   to stop cyber harassment

    b   to change the laws that govern cyber harassment and behavior on the Internet

    c   to inform readers about the problem of cyber harassment

    d   to convince the government to punish people who engage in cyber harassment

    e   to help the victims of cyber harassment

2 Choose the phrase that best describes the writer's tone regarding cyber harassment.

    a   neutral and informative

    b   positive, offering praise

    c   negative, offering criticism

7 ANNOTATING **Skim the article with your partner. Find words and phrases that support your ideas about the writer's tone and highlight or circle them. Explain your choices to another pair of students.**

☼ CRITICAL THINKING

8 **Work with a partner. Discuss the questions.**

APPLY	ANALYZE	ANALYZE
Have you ever had an experience with cyber harassment, directed either against you or someone you know? What happened?	Why do you think women are more likely to experience the most serious forms of cyber harassment?	Is it possible to stop cyber harassment completely? Why or why not?

🎲 COLLABORATION

9 **A** Work In a small group. Consider the issue of anonymity in communication. In addition to online posts, brainstorm a list of 3–4 situations where someone could remain anonymous.

    B For each situation, discuss the following questions:

      • How would anonymity be an advantage to the writer or speaker in the situation?
      • How would it be a disadvantage?

    C Reach agreement as a group on whether the advantages outweigh the disadvantages, or vice versa, in each situation. Explain your conclusions and reasons to the class.

1 USING YOUR KNOWLEDGE **You are going to read an article about possible solutions to cyber harassment. Work with a partner. Discuss the questions.**

1 The title of the article is "Combatting Cyber Harassment." What kind of solutions to cyber harassment do you think it will offer?

2 What kind of advice do you think the article will give to victims of cyber harassment?

3 Who do you think is responsible for stopping offensive behavior on the Internet?

2 UNDERSTANDING KEY VOCABULARY **Read the sentences and choose the best definition for each vocabulary item in bold.**

1 One of the players on the team was **suspended** for three games for hitting another player.

    a required to pay money as a result of doing something wrong

    b fired from one's job

    c not allowed to participate in an activity for a period of time

2 The city announced it would **prosecute** anyone who disturbed the peace during the election.

    a search for in order to arrest

    b take to court to determine the guilt of

    c commit a crime against

3   For weeks, he has been receiving **malicious** letters and phone calls, filled with lies that could destroy his career.

   a   legal but inappropriate

   b   untruthful

   c   intentionally hurtful

4   We will probably never be able to **eliminate** crime, but we can take steps to reduce it.

   a   remove; get rid of completely

   b   find an appropriate punishment for

   c   weaken significantly

5   The research institute has **assembled** a team of top scientists in an effort to find the cause of the disease.

   a   gathered

   b   attracted

   c   interviewed

6   The government imposes a **penalty** on people who do not pay their taxes on time.

   a   law

   b   punishment

   c   permission

7   The government has just passed a set of laws to help **regulate** the growing online retail market.

   a   control

   b   encourage

   c   tax

8   The inability to write well can be a **barrier** to professional success.

   a   the answer

   b   the last step

   c   something that blocks access

Combatting Cyber Harassment

1 Cyber harassment can have a serious and destructive impact on its victims and their families. Yet, until recently, it was not taken seriously. Instead, it was widely believed that this behavior was similar to childish fights, but this attitude is changing. Media attention on several recent cyber harassment cases has prompted the public to demand that trolls be held accountable for their behavior. Additionally, as offensive and often **malicious** behavior has become more prevalent, and the threats by Internet trolls have become more frightening, social media apps and sites, as well as online gaming communities, are taking notice. They worry that their users will begin to abandon their sites if trolls are allowed to operate freely. In short, taking responsibility for cyber harassment has also become an economic issue.

Prevention and Penalties

2 The effort to combat cyber harassment requires a two-pronged approach: prevention and **penalties**; however, to date, most of the focus has been on the first. Prevention can be controversial. The anonymity of the Internet makes harassment easy, yet placing any limits on online interaction could threaten the benefits of both the anonymity and free speech that we value. Online gaming communities want to provide maximum freedom to their participants, but these are the places where a great deal of harassment occurs, especially of female players. To try to address this problem, one hugely popular gaming site, *League of Legends*, **assembled** a team of behavior experts to study its 67 million monthly users.

3 What they discovered surprised them. They expected to find a small group of badly behaved players—users who were responsible for most of the abuse and hostile behavior. Their plan was to **suspend** these players in hopes of **eliminating**, or at least reducing online harassment. They did find a few "bad apples," but they discovered that most of the offensive behavior came from players who were usually good Internet citizens. They only acted badly occasionally. The research team had greater success when the chat function on the game was removed. This resulted in abusive comments dropping by 30%. This study suggests that creating even a small **barrier** to bad behavior can often stop abuse before it starts.

4 Other online communities and sites have already taken steps in this direction. Twitter has had a "report abuse" button since 2013. Some gaming sites have systems that allow players to establish their reputations in the same way that sellers on online market sites, such as eBay, must do. They rate one another as "good player" or "avoid me." In other words, the communities are beginning to **regulate** themselves. They are also using the latest technology to identify the worst offenders. Google has sponsored a research study to find an algorithm[1] for identifying them. Their posts are more frequent and generally contain negative words, poor grammar, and misspelled words, allowing researchers to identify and ban users who exhibit troll behavior.

Outdated Laws

5 Over the past few years, the federal government and about half the states in the U.S. have updated their laws to cover threats and stalking[2] over the Internet. The federal government often has to fight computer crime with laws originally written to cover the use of telephones or the Postal Service. Nevertheless, our laws still lag disturbingly behind emerging technology. What is more, so far, very few people have been **prosecuted** under the laws that do exist.

6 Experts offer advice that is familiar to anyone who has been the victim of bullying: ignore it. In reference to cyber bullying, this advice is often phrased, "Don't feed the trolls." Do not respond to the harassment. By responding to it, you give the trolls what they want—attention. Although this is generally considered to be good advice, unfortunately it often does not stop ongoing abuse.

[1]**algorithm** (n) a set of instructions to a computer
[2]**stalking** (n) illegally following someone over a period of time

7 As we spend more and more time on the Internet, addressing offensive and threatening behavior online is becoming increasingly important. As Laura Hudson wrote in *Wired* magazine in 2014, "… the Internet is now where we socialize, where we work. It's where we meet our spouses, where we build our reputations. Online harassment isn't just inconvenient, nor is it something we can walk away from with ease. It's abhorrent[3] behavior that has real social, professional, and economic costs."

Prosecuting Cyber Stalkers

Stalking occurs when someone repeatedly follows and makes unwanted contact with a victim. It becomes cyber stalking if the unwanted pursuit involves e-mail, web sites, or instant messaging. Cyber stalking is among the most serious of cybercrimes. Unfortunately, it clearly illustrates how difficult it is to prosecute cyber criminals.

In the United States, every state has an anti-stalking law, but in many states digital harassment is not clearly defined as stalking. California is among the few states that specifically say that stalking includes electronic threats or repeated electronic "following."

Some federal laws have been updated to mention electronic devices as tools in harassment. However, federal prosecutors do not generally pursue a case unless it clearly involves interstate activity. Consequently, many reported instances of cyberstalking never lead to prosecution. The state will not prosecute because of unclear legal definitions, and federal officers do not step in because the offense did not occur across state lines.

▌[3]**abhorrent** (adj) morally wrong; evil

WHILE READING

3 READING FOR MAIN IDEAS **Read the article on pages 64–66. Match each main idea to the correct paragraph.**

a   The online gaming community is taking steps to reduce abuse. _____

b   Legal measures have not been very effective. _____

c   We need to do more to fight abusive online behavior. _____

d   People are starting to take cyber harassment more seriously. _____

e   Online communities are beginning to make rules against cyber harassment. _____

4 READING FOR DETAILS **Read the article again. Complete the table with the actions that each group is taking to combat cyber harassment.**

group	actions
online gaming communities	
Twitter	
Google	
federal and state governments	

READING BETWEEN THE LINES

5 IDENTIFYING PURPOSE AND TONE **Work with a partner to complete the tasks.**

1 What are the writer's purposes? Check all that apply.

a to eliminate cyber harassment ☐

b to inform readers about current steps to stop cyber harassment ☐

c to tell readers about specific cases of cyber harassment ☐

d to help victims fight against and recover from cyber harassment ☐

e to convince readers of the need to stop cyber harassment ☐

2 Which phrase best describes the writer's tone regarding cyber harassment?

a neutral and objective ☐

b informative and argumentative ☐

c negative and emotional ☐

6 ANNOTATING **Skim the article with your partner. Find words and phrases that support your ideas about the writer's tone, and highlight or circle them. Explain your choices to another pair of students.**

⚙ CRITICAL THINKING

7 SYNTHESIZING **Work with a partner. Use ideas from Reading 1 and Reading 2 to discuss the questions.**

APPLY	ANALYZE	EVALUATE
What advice would you give to a victim of cyber crimes?	Do you think technology will find the solution to the problem? How?	What kind of penalty should people who in engage in cyber harassment face? What about for cyber stalking?

🗪 COLLABORATION

8 A Work in a small group. Research other types of cyber harassment, including doxing and swatting. Find at least two more types.

B Make a table with three columns. Each group member should fill in the following information for one type of cyber harassment:

- name
- definition / description
- examples of the harm that it can cause

C Make a poster or electronic slide of your table. Present your findings to the class. Include time for Q&A at the end of your presentation.

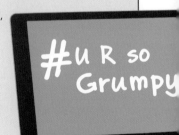

COLLOCATIONS FOR BEHAVIOR

 1 Complete each sentence with one verb (in the correct form) and one noun from the word boxes to describe behavior or responses to behavior.

verbs	nouns
build exhibit experience lose suffer take	abuse behavior confidence pain a reputation responsibility

1   When you have done something wrong, it is important to _____

_____ for your actions.

2   My online service provider has _____ _____

for protecting its users from abusive behavior.

3   People who have _____ _____ online often

decide to withdraw from any interaction at all on the Internet.

4   It is not only trolls who _____ hostile and offensive

_____ online. Some ordinary users have also been known

to act badly.

5   The stress of online abuse can cause people to _____

_____ that is both physical and psychological.

6   Even a single hostile or abusive online post can cause a user to

_____ _____ and feel bad about himself.

2 Choose three of the negative adjectives from the box below and write sentences to describe online activity, behavior, comments, or posts. Use the verb-noun collocations in Exercise 1 on page 69 where appropriate.

abhorrent	disturbing	insulting	negative	threatening
abusive	hostile	malicious	offensive	

1 _____

 _____

 _____

2 _____

 _____

 _____

3 _____

 _____

 _____

PROBLEM-SOLUTION COLLOCATIONS

LANGUAGE

There are many nouns and verbs that describe problems and solutions. Some form typical or frequent collocations.

	verbs	nouns
stating the existence of a problem	become, face	an issue
	face, pose, present, represent	a challenge, a danger, a problem, a risk, a threat
	cause, run into	trouble, problems
describing solutions	address, confront, eliminate, face, respond to	a challenge, a danger, an issue, a problem, a risk, a threat
	fix, resolve, solve	a problem
	resolve	an issue

3 Work with a partner. Read the scenarios. Retell each one to your partner, using the language in the chart on page 70 to describe the problems and solutions.

1 Two neighbors both wanted to park their cars in a space next to their apartment building. They argued about it constantly. Neighbor A had a violent temper and frightened Neighbor B, who complained to the owner of the building. The owner decided to park his own car in the space so neither neighbor could use it.

2 In the past, passengers arriving at the Houston Airport complained constantly about the length of time they had to wait for their baggage. Airport officials tried several approaches to solve the problem, including hiring extra staff. With these adjustments, the wait time was reduced to about the average at most airports, but passengers still complained. Eventually, the officials decided on a more extreme solution. They moved the baggage claim area farther away, so passengers had to walk farther to reach it.

3 A city neighborhood was having a problem with rats. The rats lived on the garbage people had thrown out. The neighbors considered using poison, but they worried about pets or even children coming into contact with it. They tried traps, but the rats were too smart. One neighbor had read about an organization that brings feral cats (wild cats that live on the streets) into neighborhoods with rat problems. The neighbors contacted the organization, which delivered five feral cats. A week later, the rats were gone. The neighbors don't think the cats killed all the rats, but those they did not kill were certainly scared away.

WATCH AND LISTEN

GLOSSARY

hack (v)   to use a computer to get into someone else's computer system or other electronic device illegally

scandal (n)   activities that shock people because they think they are very bad

breach (n)   an act of breaking a rule, law, custom, or practice

virtual fingerprint (n)   unique characteristics of a computer, file, or set of data

liable (adj)   having legal responsibility for something

PREPARING TO WATCH

1 ACTIVATING YOUR KNOWLEDGE **Take this survey about your online security habits. Check (✓) your answers. Discuss your answers with a partner.**

How safe do you feel …	Very safe	Safe	Not safe
1 sharing your address with someone?	☐	☐	☐
2 shopping online?	☐	☐	☐
3 sending private information to someone's phone?	☐	☐	☐
4 storing private information on your phone?	☐	☐	☐
5 storing passwords on your computer or phone?	☐	☐	☐

2 Discuss the questions with your partner.

1   Does everyone have a right to privacy? Why or why not?

2   Do you think celebrities and other public figures give up their right to privacy when they become famous? Why or why not?

3   What can people do to better protect their privacy?

WHILE WATCHING

▶ 3 UNDERSTANDING MAIN IDEAS **Watch the video. Write _T_ (true) or _F_ (false) next to the statements below. Correct the false statements.**

_____ 1   Apple has taken responsibility for the breach of security.

_____ 2   The FBI is looking into the case to see if they can identify the hackers.

_____ **3** The people who posted the photos are not liable and cannot be charged with breaking the law.

_____ **4** Many people feel these are cases of a sex crime.

_____ **5** People expect to have privacy in their own surroundings.

4 UNDERSTANDING DETAILS **Watch the video again. Write a detail for each main idea.**

1 These types of attacks include hackers having personal information.

_____

2 Celebrities' devices will be looked at to trace the hackers.

_____

3 The law includes penalties for hackers and for those who share the information hacked via the Internet.

_____

5 DRAWING CONCLUSIONS **Work with a partner. Discuss the questions.**

1 Why do you think hackers target celebrities?

2 What do you think motivates a hacker to invade someone's privacy?

3 How might a hacker learn a celebrity's answers to security questions?

CRITICAL THINKING

6 **Work with a partner. Discuss the questions.**

APPLY	ANALYZE	EVALUATE
What are some ways to make a password more secure?	Who do you think is responsible in hacking cases? Why?	Do you think the punishment given to Christopher Chaney was fair? Why or why not?

COLLABORATION

7 **A** Work in a group of three. Prepare a script for a news-interview TV show on the topic: *Do celebrities give up their right to privacy*? One member will be the interviewer. Another member will argue that celebrities DO give up some of their privacy. The third member will argue that celebrities have the same privacy rights as an average person

B Conduct and record a five-minute interview for the class.

C As a class, listen to each interview. Decide which side made a stronger argument.

BUSINESS

LEARNING OBJECTIVES

Key Reading Skill	Scanning
Additional Reading Skills	Using your knowledge; understanding key vocabulary; reading for main ideas; working out meaning; annotating; reading for details; making inferences; synthesizing
Language Development	Expressing contrast; business and marketing vocabulary

ACTIVATE YOUR KNOWLEDGE

Work with a partner. Discuss the questions.

1 Are there a lot of food trucks and other mobile businesses where you live? Do you ever buy from these businesses?

2 What makes you choose to shop at one business instead of another?

3 If you were going to start your own small business, what would it be? Give reasons for your answer.

PREPARING TO READ

1 USING YOUR KNOWLEDGE **You are going to read an article about mobile businesses. Do you think each statement is** *T* **(true) or** *F* **(false)?**

_____ 1   It's easy to turn a hobby into a business.

_____ 2   It is cheaper to start a food truck than a restaurant.

_____ 3   It usually only costs about $3,000 to start a mobile business.

_____ 4   New food truck owners usually make a profit more quickly than new restaurant owners.

_____ 5   The number of mobile businesses is increasing.

_____ 6   Food trucks are just a small fraction of the mobile retail market.

2 UNDERSTANDING KEY VOCABULARY **Read the definitions. Complete the sentences with the correct form of each vocabulary item in bold.**

> **aspiring** (adj)   wishing to become successful
> **break even** (v)   to earn only enough to pay expenses
> **component** (n)   one of the parts of something
> **fluctuate** (v)   to change frequently from one level to another
> **outweigh** (v)   to be greater or more important than something else
> **proposition** (n)   a proposal or suggestion, especially in business
> **revenue** (n)   the money that a business receives regularly
> **transition** (n)   a change from one state or condition to another

1   The price of oil has _____ dramatically since 2000, going from $40 a barrel to almost $150 then down to $30!

2   My friend came to me with an interesting business _____ , but I think it sounds a little too risky for me.

3   My daughter is a(n) _____ chef in New York. She hopes to get a job in a famous restaurant.

4   The benefits of this medication _____ its potential risks.

5   One _____ of the course focuses on reading comprehension and the other focuses on listening skills.

6   It can take teenagers a long time to make the _____ into adulthood.

7   The first year, our business lost money, the second year it _____ , and this year we made a profit.

8   Amazon's _____ in 2015 was over $100 billion ($100,000,000,000).

SCANNING

If you are doing research, scanning can help you find texts (especially in an Internet search) most relevant to your topic. Scanning for specific information like names and numbers, which stand out visually, is especially useful. Move your eyes quickly through the text with a search term in mind. Look for clues such as a capital letter (for a name), a number (for an amount), or a symbol (dollar sign, quotation marks, percent sign, etc.)

3 SCANNING **Scan the article on pages 78–79 to find the answers to these questions.**

1 What are average start-up costs for a food truck? _____

2 What kind of mobile business did Rich Harper start? _____

3 What are some other examples of mobile retail?

_____

4 How much did mobile retail grow between 2009 and 2014? _____

5 What are some of the problems that mobile retail owners face?

_____

6 How much money do food trucks bring in annually? _____

4 Scan the article again. Decide whether this article would be worth reading for each of these people. Write _Y_ (yes), _N_ (no), or _M_ (maybe).

1 A small business owner who wants to find a bigger location _____

2 A small business owner who wants to expand into other parts of the city but isn't sure where _____

3 A person who wants to open a restaurant but doesn't have much money _____

4 A person looking for a job with a tech company _____

5 A researcher looking for current economic trends _____

6 A researcher looking for information on traffic flow in a city _____

STARTING OUT
MOBILE

1 Maybe you make the world's best peanut butter cookies, or you've always helped your friends and neighbors by fixing their computers, or perhaps you have a green thumb and your garden is the envy of the neighborhood. A lot of businesses are started by people who have hobbies or special talents and want to turn these interests into a business. But scaling up from a hobby to a real business, such as a bakery, restaurant, or store, requires business know-how and a substantial investment. Many entrepreneurs don't have enough of either of these, so they never take the first step.

A Gradual Entry

2 An increasing number of **aspiring** business owners have found a way to take a first step that makes this **transition** from hobby to business more gradual, less expensive, and less risky. They are taking their dreams and talents on the road—in trucks. The first entrepreneurs to do this were in the food business. In recent years, a wave of food trucks have arrived on the scene, serving everything from gourmet muffins to empanadas to Korean tacos. Food trucks became a way for aspiring chefs to try out recipes and test the waters before making a big investment in a traditional, brick-and-mortar business[1].

3 Beginning on a small scale has its advantages, the most important of which is the relatively modest size of initial start-up costs. These costs, which consist primarily of the truck and any required equipment, usually come to about $20,000–$30,000, a fraction of what it would cost to start a store or restaurant. Similarly, overhead costs[2] are generally low. Mobile business owners must pay for gas, of course, but other utility payments are modest. With such tightly controlled costs, mobile businesses often **break even** in a year or two; in contrast, success comes to brick-and-mortar businesses much more slowly, and they often fail within the first two years. In short, mobile businesses are relatively low-risk **propositions**.

Beyond Food Trucks

4 The success of food trucks inspired other entrepreneurs to consider starting out on wheels. Rich Harper once ran a chain of gyms, but his real interest was boxing. In 2005, he bought an old truck, equipped it with some gym equipment, and took to the streets—all for a total start-up cost of $6,000. His business quickly turned a profit and is still going strong, as he brings the boxing ring to customers all over his state.

5 Today, there are trucks that sell flowers, shoes, clothes, and all kinds of specialty food items. There are also trucks that provide services, such as hair styling, dog grooming, and repair of high-tech devices. Mobile retail has grown steadily, posting a 12% increase between 2009 and 2014. Mobile retail is not without problems, however. Weather, the **fluctuating** price of gas, and just finding a place to park are all challenges that mobile entrepreneurs have to deal with every day. These business owners, however, feel the advantages **outweigh** the disadvantages. The mobile food business alone—the largest in the mobile retail sector—generates an average annual **revenue** of $857 million.

6 Once convinced that their business has achieved sufficient success, some successful mobile entrepreneurs move on to a brick-and-mortar business. Others, like Rich Harper and his boxing gym, are satisfied to stay mobile. In an interesting twist, some brick-and-mortar business owners, observing the success of mobile retailers, have added a mobile **component** to their business. The truck acts as a marketing tool to bring business into the store. As stand-alone businesses or as extensions of stores, mobile retail appears to be here to stay.

¹**brick-and-mortar business** (n) a business with a physical location in a building
²**overhead costs** (n) expenses that come with the physical space of a business, such as property taxes and utility payments

5 READING FOR MAIN IDEAS **Read the article on pages 78–79. What is the writer's main argument? Write your answer in one sentence. Compare ideas with a partner.**

_____

_____

_____

READING BETWEEN THE LINES

6 WORKING OUT MEANING **Scan Reading 1 again to find these phrases. Underline them, and then use context to try to understand them. Then match them to the correct meaning.**

1   (paragraph 1) have a green thumb

2   (paragraph 1) the envy of the neighborhood

3   (paragraph 1) scale up

4   (paragraph 2) arrive on the scene

5   (paragraph 2) test the waters

6   (paragraph 4) going strong

7   (paragraph 6) move on to

8   (paragraph 6) stand-alone

a   try out in a safe way or on a small scale

b   be good at growing plants

c   start becoming common

d   doing very well

e   something your neighbors wish they had

f   independent

g   take to the next level

h   exchange for (something different)

7 Work with a partner. Write a sentence for each phrase in Exercise 6, using the phrase in context correctly. Share your sentences with the class.

_____

_____

_____

_____

_____

_____

_____

_____

_____

☼ CRITICAL THINKING

8 **Work with a partner. Discuss the questions.**

APPLY	ANALYZE	EVALUATE
What role do you think social media plays in the rise of mobile retail?	In what way, if any, do you think the rise of mobile retail is related to the state of the economy?	Do you think mobile retail will continue to grow? Why or why not?

☺ COLLABORATION

9 **A** Work in a small group. Review the list of potential new businesses. Would each business work better as a mobile or traditional business?

- a yoga studio
- a tanning salon
- vintage clothing
- legal advice

- organic fruit and vegetables
- pizza
- simple medical testing

- bookselling
- children's art classes
- cell phone repair

B Use the T-chart to record your group's decisions. Give reasons for each choice. Add one more idea for a successful mobile business.

Mobile	Traditional

C Present and "sell" your new mobile business idea to the class. As a class, vote on the best new idea.

READING 2

1 USING YOUR KNOWLEDGE **You are going to read an article about customer loyalty. Check (✓) the strategies that would be successful in keeping you as a loyal customer. Then compare your choices with a partner. Discuss your reasons.**

a Special prices for loyal customers ☐

b Free shipping ☐

c A program that rewards you for buying more merchandise ☐

d Special products for loyal customers ☐

e The opportunity to buy products in high demand before the general public ☐

f Prizes or gifts ☐

2 UNDERSTANDING KEY VOCABULARY **Read the sentences and choose the best definition for each vocabulary item in bold.**

1 When gasoline prices are low, drivers have no **incentive** to leave their cars at home and take public transportation.

   a alternative

   b encouragement

   c argument

2 Some investors **shrewdly** bought property when prices were very low.

   a based on good judgment

   b based on illegal actions

   c based on luck or coincidence

3 It is important to set goals that are **attainable**; otherwise, you will just get discouraged.

   a able to be reached

   b practical; sensible

   c simple; able to be explained clearly

4 There is an **ongoing** debate in this country about the role of education in economic success.

   a formal

   b highly emotional

   c continuing

5 We have lived in this house for more than thirty years, so we have **accumulated** a lot of possessions.

    a gradually collected

    b rid ourselves of

    c increased the value of

6 The university's student **retention** rate has improved in the past ten years—almost 80% of students who start here graduate from here.

    a academic performance

    b holding; keeping

    c quality or standards

7 He was a **pioneer** in bioengineering, publishing one of the earliest studies in the field.

    a one of the first people to do something

    b one of the most famous people in a field

    c an international expert

8 After one company started to offer free shipping to its customers, other companies soon **followed suit**.

    a made a more attractive offer

    b competed against one another

    c did the same thing

REWARDS
Plus
3512 7713 8744 0000 5422   VALID THRU 09/20

Use Reward Points for Your Next Vacation!

KEEPING YOUR CUSTOMERS

1 It costs five to ten times more to sell a product to a new customer than to an existing one. So what are businesses doing to hold on to their customers? The answer is—everything they possibly can. Two popular business strategies with successful track records for customer **retention** are rewards programs, often also referred to as loyalty programs, and subscription services.

Loyalty Pays

2 Loyalty programs encourage customers to continue buying products or services from one particular company by offering customers rewards. Airlines, **pioneers** of loyalty programs, provide a good example. When customers fly with one airline on multiple trips, that airline rewards them with free travel. Generally, customers have to **accumulate** a specific number of "miles" or "points" in order to receive their reward, providing an **incentive** to continue flying with one airline. Other companies, from Starbucks to Best Buy, have **followed suit**, offering rewards to loyal customers.

3 American consumers often belong to multiple loyalty programs, yet most people participate actively in only a few. Companies are interested in understanding the reasons behind this behavior. The most successful loyalty programs have several features in common. They are simple and easy to understand, but most important, their rewards are **attainable**. Customers receive rewards often enough that they see the benefit of remaining loyal to the company. The programs not only keep customers buying the company's products or services, they also provide the company with valuable information about their customers' behavior and preferences.

LOYALTY PAYS

> **American consumers often belong to multiple loyalty programs, yet most people participate actively in only a few.**

Subscription Services

4 A second successful strategy for maintaining customer relationships is the subscription service. In these programs customers sign up to purchase items, such as shaving products, snacks, or makeup, on a regular basis. These items are delivered to the customer's home. The convenience of home delivery is an idea with a long history, but subscription services offer more than a convenient way to replace household necessities. They offer customers products that are tailored to their own personal needs and desires. This kind of treatment makes customers feel special and deepens their connection

to the brand. In a retail environment where consumers are faced with a dizzying array of products, this kind of service can combat what has been referred to as "the paralysis of choice." In other words, the service makes decisions for consumers who may have difficulty making decisions for themselves. For the company, subscription services offer guaranteed regular sales, an **ongoing** relationship with their customers, and, like loyalty programs, a rich source of data about buying behavior.

> ❝ **Subscription services offer customers products that are tailored to their own personal needs and desires.** ❞

5 Some companies, such as Amazon, even charge their customers for their subscription service. In return, customers get what they value most, for example, free shipping or access to digital content. It may seem as if Amazon would lose money by not charging their customers for shipping, but the company has **shrewdly** calculated that customers, having paid for the subscription service, will shop on Amazon even for items they might otherwise buy at the local supermarket. One study showed that Amazon subscription customers spent an average of $1,500 per year, compared to non-subscription customers, who spent just $625.

6 Rewards programs and subscription services are just two of the marketing tools that businesses use to hold on to customers. They have learned that it makes better business sense to devote attention and even money to their current customers than to try to attract new ones.

WHILE READING

3 READING FOR MAIN IDEAS **Read the article on pages 84–86. Which of these statements are consistent with the claims made there? Compare your answers with a partner.**

a Businesses are less concerned with keeping customers than with finding new ones. ☐

b Rewards programs are a good way to keep customers loyal. ☐

c Customers will not participate in loyalty programs if the goals are too hard to reach. ☐

d The main reason customers participate in subscription programs is the low price of joining them. ☐

e Subscription services are more successful than loyalty programs in attracting and keeping customers. ☐

f Subscription programs can increase sales. ☐

4 ANNOTATING **For each statement, underline the sentence in the article with a similar meaning.**

1 Businesses are doing everything possible to keep their customers. (Paragraph 1)

2 This idea is illustrated by airlines, which were among the first kinds of businesses to use these programs. (Paragraph 2)

3 A successful loyalty program is not too complicated and offers rewards that people can reach. (Paragraph 3)

4 Customers have known for a long time that it's convenient to have products delivered to their homes. (Paragraph 4)

5 Amazon has figured out that offering free shipping to subscribers pays off by making sure they buy things through Amazon, not elsewhere. (Paragraph 5)

6 Businesses have many marketing strategies beyond rewards and subscriptions. (Paragraph 6)

5 READING FOR DETAILS **Scan the article to find the information to complete these paragraphs.**

The most effective loyalty programs are (1)_____ and have (2)_____ rewards. Keeping customers loyal is not the only reason for such programs. They also provide (3)_____ information about what (4)_____ like. (5)_____ were the first to offer rewards programs, and they are probably still the most familiar to the public.

Subscription services offer more than (6)_____ ; they also offer products that are specific to customers' needs and (7)_____ . They offer a limited selection, which helps customers make (8)_____ . Research suggests that customers buy more products when they have a subscription. Amazon subscription members spend an average of (9)_____ per year, compared to non-subscription customers, who spend only about (10)_____ .

READING BETWEEN THE LINES

6 MAKING INFERENCES **Work with a partner. Discuss the questions.**

1 How do you think loyalty programs provide companies with data on customer behavior?

2 Why might customers join a loyalty program but then not participate actively in it?

3 What does the term *the paralysis of choice* mean?

4 Why might products such as snacks, razors for shaving, and makeup be popular items for subscription services?

⌖ CRITICAL THINKING

7 SYNTHESIZING **Work with a partner. Use ideas from Reading 1 and Reading 2 to discuss the questions.**

APPLY	APPLY	ANALYZE
Do you participate in a loyalty program? If so, what do you like or not like about it? If not, why not?	Do you participate in a subscription service? If so, do you think having the subscription has encouraged you to buy more? If not, why not?	Why do you think it is so much easier to hold on to existing customers than to attract new ones?

🖧 COLLABORATION

8 **A** Work in a small group. One type of online subscription service is *curated shopping*. Find a definition.

B Make a list of five types of products or services provided by curated shopping. For each product or service on your list, discuss the advantages and disadvantages of using curated shopping. Record your ideas.

C Share your lists and ideas with another group. Come to agreement on the best use of curated shopping. Repeat step C with other groups.

EXPRESSING CONTRAST

LANGUAGE

There are many different ways to signal contrasting ideas. Contrast signals may differ in both structure and meaning.

Structure

Unlike other companies, Amazon charges for its subscription service.
Many subscription services are free; Amazon, **by contrast**, charges a substantial fee for its program.

Meaning

Contrast signals typically express one of three somewhat different meanings.

	prepositions	transition word or phrase
direct contrast	unlike in contrast to	by contrast however on the other hand
concession: to show that the contrast might not be complete or is unexpected	despite in spite of	nevertheless yet however
correction or replacement: to show that the first clause or phrase is wrong or insufficient and that the clause that follows is correct	instead of rather than	instead on the contrary in fact rather however

1 **Read the sentences. Choose the best contrast signal. Pay attention to structure and meaning.**

1 _____ the convenience of subscription services, these programs are not as popular as loyalty programs.

   a Instead of   **b** In spite of   **c** Nevertheless

2 One company has decided to avoid the whole point system in their loyalty program. _____ , they give their loyal customers their rewards immediately.

   a Instead   **b** However   **c** On the other hand

3 About a quarter of all new restaurants fail in their first year. _____ , hundreds of entrepreneurs open restaurants every year, hoping to beat the odds.

   a Rather   **b** Despite   **c** Nevertheless

4 _____ loyalty programs, subscription programs restrict membership to special customers, giving those customers the sense that they belong to an exclusive club.

   a Unlike   **b** Instead of   **c** However

5 Mobile businesses are not as risky as they seem; _____ , they are less likely to lose money than brick-and-mortar businesses.

   a by contrast   **b** in fact   **c** on the other hand

BUSINESS AND MARKETING VOCABULARY

2 **Complete the information about business and marketing with the correct form of the words and phrases from the box.**

> break even   brick-and-mortar
> generate revenue   marketing tool
> on a large/small scale   start-up costs
> track record   turn a profit   utilities

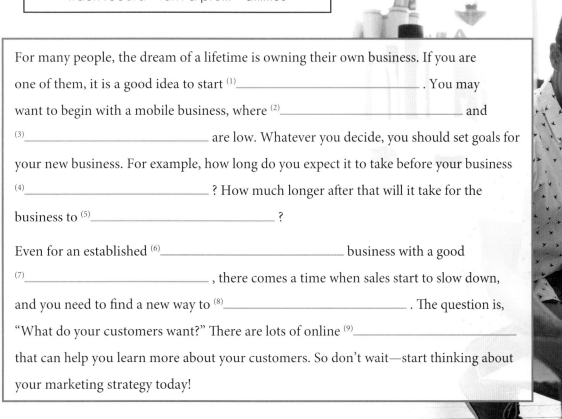

For many people, the dream of a lifetime is owning their own business. If you are one of them, it is a good idea to start (1)_____ . You may want to begin with a mobile business, where (2)_____ and (3)_____ are low. Whatever you decide, you should set goals for your new business. For example, how long do you expect it to take before your business (4)_____ ? How much longer after that will it take for the business to (5)_____ ?

Even for an established (6)_____ business with a good (7)_____ , there comes a time when sales start to slow down, and you need to find a new way to (8)_____ . The question is, "What do your customers want?" There are lots of online (9)_____ that can help you learn more about your customers. So don't wait—start thinking about your marketing strategy today!

WATCH AND LISTEN

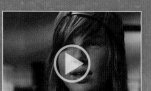   

GLOSSARY

foreclosure (n)   the act of taking back property that was bought with borrowed money because the money was not paid as agreed

garage sale (n)   an occasion when people sell things they no longer want but feel someone else might want; often done in a garage

attention deficit hyperactivity disorder (ADHD) (n)   a condition in which someone, especially a child, is often in a state of activity or excitement and unable to direct their attention toward what they are doing

deed (n)   a legal document that is an official record and proof of ownership of property

take stock (v)   to examine a situation carefully

PREPARING TO WATCH

1 ACTIVATING YOUR KNOWLEDGE **Work with a partner. Discuss the questions.**

1   What are typical things that teenagers like to do?

2   What are some of the ways that teenagers can earn money where you live?

3   Do you know a teenager who owns a business? What kind of business?

2 PREDICTING CONTENT USING VISUALS **Look at the pictures from the video. Discuss the questions with your partner.**

1   What activities do you think the teenage girl likes?

2   What kind of business do you think she has?

3   How much money do you think she earns?

WHILE WATCHING

3 UNDERSTANDING MAIN IDEAS **Watch the video. Check (✓) the ideas you hear.**

1   Willow is a landlord. ☐

2   Willow has sold household items for money to buy houses. ☐

3   Once Willow is a legal adult, the properties will belong to her. ☐

4   Willow has a goal of owning 10 houses by the time she is 18. ☐

5   Willow plans to become a realtor. ☐

4 UNDERSTANDING DETAILS **Watch the video again. Write a detail for each main idea.**

1 Willow made a good deal of money selling furniture, allowing her to buy her first home.

_____

2 Her goal is to buy two houses a year.

_____

3 Willow's mother is helping her.

_____

4 Willow participates in many tasks as a landlord and business owner.

_____

5 MAKING INFERENCES **Work with a partner. Discuss the questions.**

1 What do you think Willow is learning as a landlord and business owner?

2 Why do you think Willow wanted to start a business?

3 Why do you think her mother is so proud of her?

☀ CRITICAL THINKING

6 Work with a partner. Discuss the questions.

UNDERSTAND	APPLY	ANALYZE
How would you describe Willow? Why?	What could other teenagers learn from Willow?	How might Willow use the principles behind mobile businesses and customer-retention techniques to expand her business?

☙ COLLABORATION

7 A Work in a small group. How do you feel about teens in the business world? Discuss the following questions:

- Is it always culturally acceptable for teens to be businesspeople?
- Is business ownership a good use of a teen's time and energy?
- What risks do teen businesspeople face?
- Do the benefits of being in business outweigh the risks?
- Are some businesses better for teen ownership than others?
- What resources do teens need to get into business for themselves?

B Reach agreement on six to eight basic principles for teen business ownership. Create a one-page flyer that gives advice to teens about going into business. Share your flyer with the class.

PSYCHOLOGY

LEARNING OBJECTIVES

Key Reading Skills	Using graphic organizers to take notes; interpreting quotes
Additional Reading Skills	Understanding key vocabulary; previewing; taking notes; making inferences; predicting content using visuals; reading for main ideas; reading for details; synthesizing
Language Development	Experimental science vocabulary; complex noun phrases with *what*

ACTIVATE YOUR KNOWLEDGE

Work with a partner. Discuss the questions.

1 Who is the person in the photo? What do you know about her?

2 Do you consider yourself a creative person? Why or why not? What does it mean to be creative?

3 Name three famous people, living or dead, whom you consider to be creative geniuses. In what ways are such people different from the rest of the population? What do they have that most people don't? Explain your answer.

PREPARING TO READ

1 UNDERSTANDING KEY VOCABULARY **You are going to read an article about mental illness and creativity. Read the definitions. Complete the sentences with the correct form of each vocabulary item in bold.**

> GLOSSARY
>
> **intriguing** (adj)   very interesting; mysterious
>
> **label** (v)   to assign a (usually negative) characteristic to someone or something
>
> **norm** (n)   accepted standard or way of doing something
>
> **notion** (n)   idea
>
> **pursue** (v)   to try to do something over a period of time
>
> **reject** (v)   to refuse to accept
>
> **skeptical** (adj)   doubting that something is true
>
> **suppress** (v)   to prevent something from being expressed or known

1 She tried to _____ all her other thoughts in order to concentrate completely on the exam questions.

2 This kind of behavior is definitely not the _____ for animals that live in the wild, but an animal's behavior often changes when it lives in a zoo.

3 Most people are _____ of the stories about a monster that lives in the lake.

4 In spite of the substantial proof that our climate is getting warmer, some people still _____ the idea.

5 The _____ that the Earth is round actually goes back as far as 8,000 years ago.

6 The results of this study on creative thinking are _____ , but more research will be required to confirm them.

7 If you always complain and don't work well with others, you will be _____ as an unsatisfactory employee.

8 She's majoring in biology because she wants to _____ a career in medical research and neuroscience.

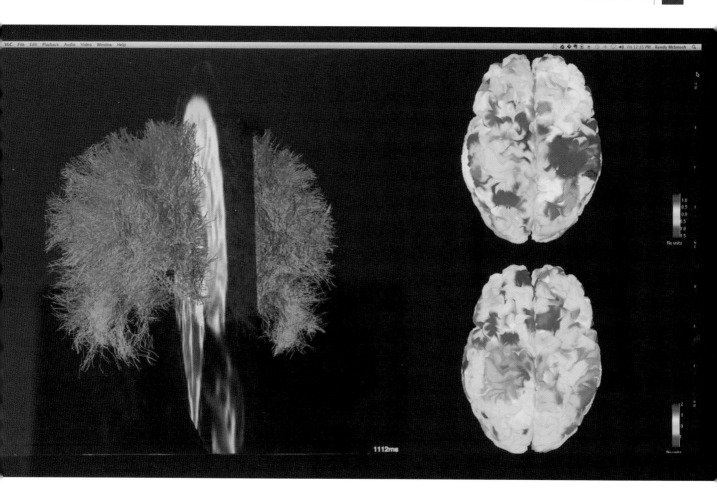

2 PREVIEWING **Read the first sentence of each paragraph of the article on pages 98–99. Then check (✓) the topics you think will be discussed in the article. Compare answers with a partner.**

a   the history of the connection between mental illness and creativity ☐

b   the causes of certain types of mental illness ☐

c   different points of view on the connection between mental illness and creativity ☐

d   how psychologists test people to determine if they are suffering from mental illness ☐

e   results of research studies on the connection between mental illness and creativity ☐

f   how experts define both creativity and mental illness ☐

3 After you read the article, check your predictions in Exercise 2.

Mental Illness and Creative Genius: Is There a Connection?

Van Gogh self-portrait (1889)

[1]**tortured** (adj) deeply troubled
[2]**mood disorder** (n) psychological problems that involve extreme emotions
[3]**rigorous** (adj) strict; of a high standard

1 The association of mental illness with creative genius goes back to ancient times. The Greeks considered creative but troubled geniuses to be "touched by the gods." The list of tortured[1] artists throughout history is both long and familiar. It includes writers such as Hemingway, Tolstoy, and Woolf, painters such as Gauguin, Van Gogh, and Kahlo, and musicians such as Mozart, Billie Holiday, and Kurt Cobain, to name just a few. Some artists report their own mental illness as crucial to their creative process while others curse their struggles. Van Gogh, in a letter to his brother, writes, "Oh, if I could have worked without this accursed disease—what things I might have done."

2   The scientific community is divided on what role, if any, mental illness plays in creativity. Several important early studies tried to establish this link. In the 1970s, neuroscientist Nancy Andreasen conducted a study of 30 well-known writers and found that 80% of them had experienced a major episode of mood disorder[2], compared with 30% of her control group. A subsequent study of 47 famous British writers and artists reported a lower, but still significant, percentage reporting mood disorders.

3   These early studies were on a small scale and relied on interviews and self-reported behavior. More recent studies have been much larger and more scientifically rigorous[3]. In these studies, the connection found between creativity and mental illness has been weaker, yet, the authors argue, still important and worth **pursuing**. These studies suggest a genetic basis for both creativity and some forms of mental illness, pointing to a possible connection. Commenting on one of the largest studies, neurologist Dr. Kari Stefansson observed in a 2015 interview in *The Guardian*, "Often, when people are creating something new, they end up straddling … sanity and insanity."

4   Nevertheless, other members of the scientific community are **skeptical** of the association between creativity and mental illness, calling this a romantic, 19th-century **notion**. They stress the fact that most mentally ill individuals are not particularly creative, and most creative artists are in good mental health. Furthermore, they point out that creative artists who do suffer from mental illness usually work more effectively when their conditions are treated and controlled. They argue that any connection between mental illness and creativity may be the result of purely practical factors. People who don't fit in with societal **norms** and tend to think and act differently, perhaps even enough to be **labeled** mentally ill, may be attracted to a life in the arts, where their behavior is more likely to be accepted, or at least tolerated.

> **❝**
> **Often, when people are creating something new, they end up straddling… sanity and insanity.**

5   Still, even those who **reject** the notion of any direct or causal connection admit that creative artists and those who suffer from some forms of mental illness may share some characteristics. One recent study that compared these two groups revealed an **intriguing** result. Both populations showed high measures of one specific type of behavior: the inability to **suppress** competing stimuli and cognitive activity while focusing on a central task. In other words, they had difficulty performing the assigned task—remembering sequences of numbers—when they were presented with other information on a screen at the same time. They could not stop themselves from paying attention to this additional information. In 2013, psychologist Barry Kaufman, writing in a blog in the journal *Scientific American*, summarizes the study's findings this way, "It seems that the key to creative cognition is opening up the floodgates and letting in as much information as possible. Because you never know: sometimes the most bizarre associations can turn into the most productively creative ideas."

6   As the results of studies like these emerge, the scientific community will continue to debate the connection between mental health and creative thinking. In the public imagination, however, the notion persists that the creative genius straddles sanity and insanity.

4 TAKING NOTES **Read the article on pages 98–99. Fill in the chart with information that supports the two sides of the issue presented in the article. Then compare your notes with a partner.**

Connection between mental illness and creativity

yes	no
1970s study found 80% of subjects had mood disorders	most creative people are not mentally ill

READING BETWEEN THE LINES

5 MAKING INFERENCES Work with a partner. Read each quotation and write your interpretation. Why do you think the writer included this quote in the text? Read the article again for context, if needed. Look up any words you don't know, especially the words in bold.

source	quote	your interpretation
Stefansson	"… when people are creating something new, they end up **straddling** … sanity and insanity." (paragraph 3)	
Kaufman	"… the key to creative cognition is opening up the **floodgates** and letting in as much information as possible." (paragraph 5)	

✧ CRITICAL THINKING

6 Work with a partner. Discuss the questions.

APPLY

What do you think is the source of creativity? Can it be taught or learned?

APPLY

Do you know of someone who has psychological problems and who is also very creative? Describe this person.

ANALYZE

Why do you think people with psychological problems are more likely to be tolerated in a community of artists?

COLLABORATION

7 **A** Work with a partner. Do a similar experiment to the one described in Reading 1. Choose an online video about a subject that interests you. The video should be informative, not just entertaining.

B Start the video. As you watch and listen to the video, count backwards from 100 by twos (100, 98, 96, 94…). Continue counting even if you make mistakes. Your partner should keep track of your progress.

C Switch roles and repeat step B. Discuss your performances and relate them to the ideas in paragraph 5 of the article.

D Report the results of your experiment and your explanations to the class.

PREPARING TO READ

1 PREDICTING CONTENT USING VISUALS You are going to read an article about creativity. Work in small groups. Complete the task. How do you think this task relates to creativity?

Imagine that you have only these items: a candle, a box of matches, and some thumbtacks.

Using only these items, how would you attach the candle to the wall so that the melting wax will not drip onto anything below it? (answer on page 174)

2 UNDERSTANDING KEY VOCABULARY Read the sentences and choose the best definition for each vocabulary item in bold.

1   I'm such a **procrastinator**. Whenever I have to write a paper, I always end up finishing it just hours before the deadline.

    a   a person who worries a lot

    b   a person who always makes excuses for mistakes

    c   a person who waits as long as possible to begin work

2   The students receive a lot of intellectual **stimulation** at this school. They are encouraged to explore their world and try new things.

    a   things that arouse interest

    b   educational opportunity and activity

    c   help with difficult things

3 The government is **seeking** new ways to create more employment opportunities.

   a starting to develop

   b gathering information about

   c trying to find

4 The speaker's words **triggered** an angry reaction from the crowd.

   a caused

   b described

   c softened

5 A government spokesman **confirmed** that two people had been hurt in the attack.

   a reported a suspicion

   b stated that something is true

   c denied that something is true

6 Engineers often have to be very **resourceful**, using whatever is available to solve problems.

   a able to find and use different ways to achieve goals

   b able to save time, money, and energy

   c able to understand complex problems quickly

7 Scientists announced that they had made a **breakthrough** in their understanding of the development of cancer cells.

   a important discovery

   b research tool

   c new way of describing something

8 He decided to use an **innovative** approach to teaching science because more traditional approaches had been ineffective.

   a based on research

   b highly structured

   c new and different

The Creative Mind

1 What is the secret to the world's most creative minds—the minds of **resourceful** inventors, **innovative** scientists, and inspired artists? Such individuals are certainly intelligent, but intelligence cannot be the key, as numerous studies have shown that a high IQ alone does not lead to creativity. …

More information

FOLLOWERS
201k

ELSEWHERE

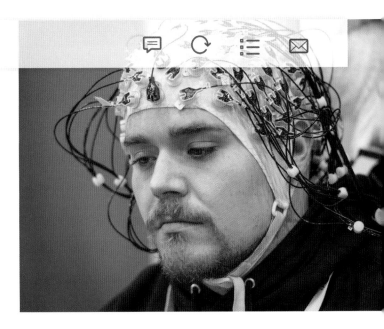

... Creative thinkers seem to have a special way of thinking. Creativity researcher and neuroscientist Nancy Andreasen, in a 2014 *Atlantic* magazine article, describes creative people as "better at recognizing relationships, making associations and connections, and seeing things in an original way—seeing things that others cannot see." For example, in the early 2000s, Jack Dorsey, one of the founders of Twitter, tried to use text alerts to improve the system for reserving and sending out taxis. He made a connection between two seemingly unrelated systems, but he was too far ahead of his time—the necessary technology was not yet available. Today, most taxi services use a version of Dorsey's original idea.

2 So what are the requirements for creativity? Psychologists contend that there are actually two levels of creative thinking which they refer to as "Big C" and "small c." Big C creativity applies to **breakthrough** ideas, ones that may change the course of a field or even history. Small c creativity refers to everyday creative problem-solving, which psychologists subdivide further into convergent and divergent thinking. Convergent thinking involves examining all of the facts and arriving at a single solution. In contrast, divergent thinking involves coming up with many possible solutions, for example, thinking of many different uses for a brick or paper clip. What most people think of as creativity generally involves divergent thinking.

3 Andreasen and others investigating the sources of creativity have noted that small c creativity does not always lead to Big C breakthroughs. True creative geniuses seem to have additional characteristics, ones that do not always fit in well with societal norms. These people seem wired[1] to **seek** novelty, take risks, and push limits in their explorations. The reward centers in their brains seem to need more than the average amount of **stimulation** in order to release dopamine, the chemical that **triggers** feelings of pleasure. As children, they were often unable to sit still, unable to focus on their lessons, instead, always looking for something new and interesting to capture their attention. Today, children who display this kind of behavior are often labeled ADHD[2] because they cause problems in the classroom. These same characteristics were probably extremely useful in the past—when humans depended on hunting, a risky and unpredictable but exciting activity—and researchers suspect they may also contribute to creativity.

> **True creative geniuses seem to have additional characteristics, ones that do not always fit in well with societal norms."**

Martin Luther King, Jr., at work in his study

4 Creativity, with a big or small c, takes time. We tend to think of breakthroughs as coming in a sudden flash of genius, but this is rarely the case. Ideas often evolve and form over a long period. Andreasen, referring to her study of creative thinking, described her findings this way, "… almost all of my subjects **confirmed** that when eureka moments[3] occur, they tend to be precipitated by long periods of preparation and incubation[4], and to strike when the mind is relaxed." In fact, many of history's most creative people have a reputation as **procrastinators.** Martin Luther King, Jr., reportedly wrote his "I Have a Dream" speech at ten o'clock the night before he delivered it, though it had most likely gone through a long period of "preparation and incubation" in his mind before that.

5 The search for the source of creativity continues. Most researchers agree that the answer will be complex and that there is probably no single characteristic, no single secret to explain the world's most creative minds.

[1] **wired** (adj) biologically programmed
[2] **ADHD** (n) Attention Deficit Hyperactivity Disorder
[3] **eureka moment** (n) the point at which you suddenly understand the answer or solution to a problem
[4] **incubation** (n) protected development

 57   11 replies

WHILE READING

3 READING FOR MAIN IDEAS AND DETAILS **Read the article on pages 104–106. Write *MI* (main idea), *SD* (supporting detail), or *X* (information not given) next to the statements.**

1   Creative people have a special way of thinking. _____

2   Andreasen's research explores the connection between intelligence and creativity. _____

3   Divergent thinking means finding many different ways to solve a problem.

_____

4   Creative thinkers seek new experiences. _____

5   The painter Van Gogh was known to take a lot of risks. _____

6   Some aspects of creative behavior may have been beneficial to early humans.

_____

7   Creative thinking is often a slow process. _____

8   Many creative people also procrastinate. _____

4 **Read the article again. Take notes about creativity by filling in details in this graphic organizer.**

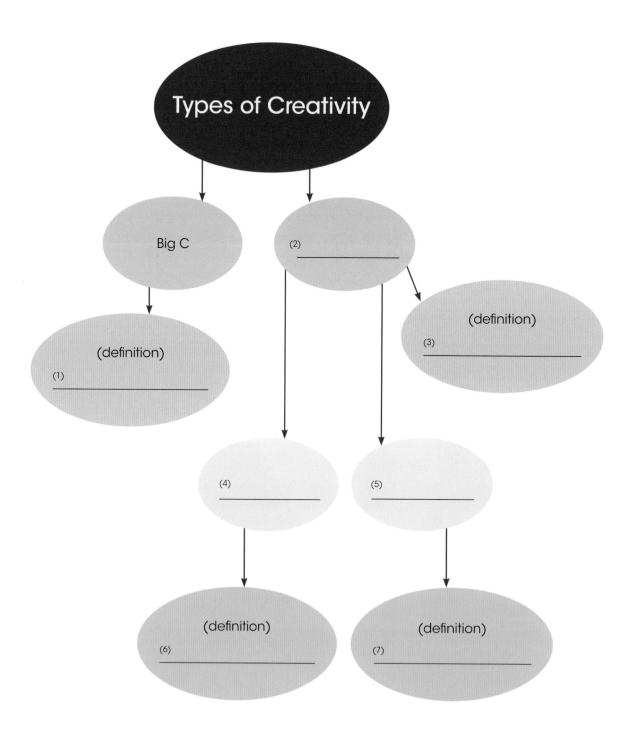

Types of Creativity

Big C

(2) _____

(definition)
(1) _____

(definition)
(3) _____

(4) _____

(5) _____

(definition)
(6) _____

(definition)
(7) _____

READING BETWEEN THE LINES

5 MAKING INFERENCES **Work in a small group. Discuss the questions.**

1 How does the example of Jack Dorsey illustrate creativity?

2 How is procrastination related to the concept of incubation?

3 Why might an early human with ADHD have been a good hunter?

☼ CRITICAL THINKING

6 SYNTHESIZING **Work with a partner. Use ideas from Reading 1 and Reading 2 to discuss the questions.**

APPLY	ANALYZE	EVALUATE
Are you more of a convergent or divergent thinker? Why?	What different kinds of tasks or professions are more appropriate for convergent thinkers? For divergent thinkers? Why?	Think of a behavior that used to be acceptable but is now labeled abnormal, or even a sign of mental illness. Why do you think it was acceptable in the past but not now?

✿ COLLABORATION

7 A Work in a small group. Do some research to find out the inspiration for some famous achievements, and complete the chart. The first one has been done as an example.

name (job)	achievement	inspiration
Archimedes (physicist)	the principle of buoyancy	*taking a bath*
Isaac Newton (physicist)	the law of gravity	
Philo T. Farnsworth (inventor)	television screens	
George de Mestral (inventor)	Velcro	
Paul McCartney (musician)	the song "Yesterday"	

B Choose one line from the chart for additional research. On a large piece of paper or poster, create a visual story of the creative achievement. Think about:

- How it was inspired
- How the creator reacted to the inspiration
- How the creator refined the inspiration to make a successful product
- How the creation was received by other people

C Use your poster to tell the class about the inspired creation you chose.

EXPERIMENTAL SCIENCE TERMINOLOGY

 1 **Read the summary of a child development study. Write the words and phrases in bold next to their definitions below.**

> A study that began in 1986 **established a causal link** between the behavior of parents and the success of their children. The **research subjects** in this study were the families of 129 children living in poverty in Jamaica. There were two **experimental groups**, and each group received a different treatment. In one, the children received extra food and milk. In the other, the families received visits from an expert in early childhood development, who encouraged the parents to spend more time engaged with their children: reading books, singing songs, or simply playing. A third set of families, the **control group**, received no treatment. The experiment lasted for two years, but the researchers who **conducted the study** continued to follow the children.
>
> The researchers found that the **intervention** that made the most difference in the children's lives was early parental interaction. As they were growing up, the children in this group exhibited more positive behavior and had higher IQ scores than the children in the other groups. As adults, they earned 25% more than the other participants in the study. The researchers **contend** that their results have clear **implications**. To ensure the future success of children living in poverty, educate parents about the importance of parent–child interaction.

1 _____ (v) to do academic research, such as an experiment

2 _____ (n) action taken to deal with a problem

3 _____ (n) conclusions suggested by the results of an academic study

4 _____ (n) participants in an experiment who do not receive experimental treatment

5 _____ (n) participants in an experiment who receive experimental treatment

6 _____ (n) all the participants in an experiment

7 _____ (v) to show a cause-and-effect connection

8 _____ (v) to claim

COMPLEX NOUN PHRASES WITH *WHAT*

A complex noun phrase with *what* can perform the same function as a noun + relative clause.

In a complex noun phrase beginning with *what*, the pronoun *what* replaces both the relative pronoun and the noun (phrase) it refers to. However, *what* can only be used to replace general terms like "the things/stuff/activities that ..."

These complex noun phrases can appear as subjects or objects. Notice that, although "the things/stuff/activities" are plural, *what* always takes a singular verb.

Subject: **What most people think of as creativity** generally involves divergent thinking.

Object: The quiet environment and free time gave him exactly **what he needed** in order to think creatively.

Complex noun phrases with *what* add variety to a writer's sentences. This structure is also an efficient and elegant way to draw attention to a point.

2 Rewrite the sentences so that they contain a complex noun phrase with *what*. Make sure to use the correct verb form after what.

1   The articles describe the activities that the research subjects in the study did in order to demonstrate their creativity.

_____

_____

2   The things that have long been considered signs of mental illness may actually be part of the creative process.

_____

_____

3   We still don't know for certain the things that lead to creativity.

_____

_____

4   The researchers were looking for the things that single out the most creative people in the population.

_____

_____

5   One of the goals of the study was to find out the activities that creative people are doing when they come up with their best ideas.

_____

_____

WATCH AND LISTEN

GLOSSARY

breakthrough idea (n)   an important or novel idea that helps to improve a situation or provide an answer to a problem

opt out (v)   to choose not to be part of an activity or to stop being involved in it

foster (v)   to encourage the development or growth of something

curator (n)   a person in charge of a department of a museum or other place where objects of art, of science, or from the past are collected, or a person who organizes and arranges a showing of art or other objects of interest

empathy (n)   the ability to share someone else's feelings or experiences by imagining what it would be like to be in that person's situation

PREPARING TO WATCH

1 ACTIVATING YOUR KNOWLEDGE **Work with a partner. Discuss the questions.**

1 Do you think people are born creative or is creativity learned? Why do you think so?

2 What are some ways creativity can be encouraged? What are some ways it is inhibited?

3 Is creativity an important factor in your choice of career? Why or why not?

2 Check (✓) the statements you agree with. Discuss your answers with a partner.

1 All children are creative. ☐

2 Creativity is a talent, like playing the piano well or being good with numbers. ☐

3 Many occupations require creativity. ☐

4 Other people influence how creative we think we are. ☐

5 Creativity can be fostered and developed. ☐

WHILE WATCHING

(▶) **3** UNDERSTANDING MAIN IDEAS **Watch the video. Circle the correct answer.**

1 What is creative confidence?

   a following new ideas without the fear of being judged

   b being brave enough to pursue your own innovative ideas

   c understanding your own particular kind of creativity

2 Why do many people stop believing they are creative?

    a They do not like being judged as creative or not.

    b A teacher told them that they are not very creative.

    c They are not good at drawing.

3 According to David Kelley, what is the real key to developing creativity?

    a understanding the needs of the people you want to create for

    b exploring the ideas of those in the technology and business fields

    c determining why something is meaningful to you

▶ **4** SUMMARIZING **Watch the video again. Then complete the summary with one or two words in each space.**

The Kelley brothers have used their creativity to (1)_____ many everyday objects. Their book, *Creative Confidence*, has been helping many people develop and foster their own creativity. While interviewing 100 people, they (2)_____ that people have ideas, they just hold those ideas in. Being told that you are not creative has resulted in people (3)_____. Creativity needs to be (4)_____, just like playing the piano. People can enhance their creativity by building (5)_____ for people. Once this happens, (6)_____ ideas can emerge.

💡 CRITICAL THINKING

5 **Discuss the questions with your partner.**

APPLY

How have other people affected your creative confidence?

ANALYZE

How can courage be fostered in young people?

EVALUATE

Do you agree that empathy is the key to creativity? Why or why not?

🤝 COLLABORATION

6 A Work in a small group. In every culture there are obstacles to creativity. Choose one culture that you know well. Brainstorm a list of ten factors that limit the creativity of people in that culture.

    B Come to agreement on the five most important factors. For each factor, find examples of creative people who are negatively affected.

    C Report your findings to the class. Provide clear explanations, examples, and visuals in your report.

CAREERS

LEARNING OBJECTIVES

Key Reading Skill	Interpreting graphical information
Additional Reading Skills	Understanding key vocabulary; predicting content using visuals; reading for main ideas; reading for details; annotating; identifying purpose and tone; making inferences; synthesizing
Language Development	Complex noun phrases

ACTIVATE YOUR KNOWLEDGE

Work with a partner. Discuss the questions.

1   What is happening in this picture? Have you experienced something similar?

2   What do you think is the main purpose of a college education?

3   Is college the best choice for everyone? Why or why not? What other options are there?

PREPARING TO READ

1 UNDERSTANDING KEY VOCABULARY **Read the definitions. Complete the sentences with the correct form of each vocabulary item in bold.**

> **alternative** (adj)   different from what is usual
>
> **assertive** (adj)   forceful; bold and confident
>
> **boast** (v)   to talk proudly about; to have or own something to be proud of
>
> **expertise** (n)   a high level of knowledge or skill
>
> **persistent** (adj)   strong and determined; lasting for a long time and difficult to resolve
>
> **prospective** (adj)   possible, especially in the future
>
> **qualified** (adj)   having the necessary knowledge or skill
>
> **survey** (n)   a set of questions asked of a large number of people in order to find patterns

1   Professors at this technical institute are known for their _____ in robotics and high-tech electronics.

2   It was difficult to fill the position in IT because most of the applicants really weren't _____ for the job.

3   We are conducting a _____ to find out how happy customers are with their purchases.

4   Our new campus _____ a brand new computer and technology center as well as a career placement service.

5   You have to be more _____ if you want people to take your ideas seriously.

6   Our shipping costs are way too high, so we are looking for _____ ways to deliver goods to our customers.

7   The staff in the admissions office regularly meet with _____ students to answer their questions and give campus tours.

8   For the last five years, there has been a _____ shortage of job applicants with skills in a wide range of technical areas.

SKILLS

INTERPRETING GRAPHICAL INFORMATION

Academic texts often include charts, graphs, or other graphical elements to support and extend the content of the text.

As a first step to understanding information presented in graphical form, read the title, headings, and the labels on the axes of any graphs. This will provide some context for the information presented there. If the axes of a graph are not labeled, try to figure out what the labels would be.

2 PREDICTING CONTENT USING VISUALS **You are going to read an article about the demand for workers with appropriate skills for current and future jobs. Work with a partner. Look at the graph below and discuss the questions.**

1 What kinds of jobs does each category include? Name some.

_____

_____

2 What sorts of skills and education are required for the jobs in these fields?

_____

_____

3 Why do you think these occupational areas are predicted to be the fastest growing in the near future?

_____

_____

4 What implications might this prediction have for curriculum development in middle and high schools?

_____

_____

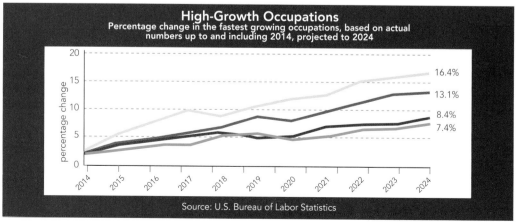

3 Now look at the graphs in Reading 1 on pages 119–121 and complete the table.

	figure 1	figure 2
What does the horizontal axis (the x axis) measure?		
What does the vertical axis (the y axis) measure?		
What information does the whole graph express?	Since 2006,	Since 2011,

4 Review the information in the graphs in Reading 1 and answer the questions.

1 Look at Figure 1. Why do you think companies are having trouble finding employees?

_____

2 What problem does Figure 2 illustrate?

_____

3 How does the information in Figure 2 explain the problems that the employers in Figure 1 are experiencing?

_____

_____

_____

THE SKILLS GAP

1 All over the country, business leaders and government officials complain about the "skills gap." Businesses have plenty of job openings, but they cannot find enough **qualified** applicants to fill the positions because workers' skills do not match those needed by employers. Figure 1 shows the results of an annual **survey** of about 42,000 companies worldwide.

2 For the most part, the employees that employers are seeking fall into two categories. The first category includes professionals in STEM fields (science / technology / engineering / mathematics) that require advanced training and **expertise**, especially in information technology (IT). The second category is much larger, comprising workers in the "skilled trades." Workers in the skilled trades have expertise in, for example, manufacturing, computers, electronics, and construction. There are simply not enough workers with training in these areas to meet the growing demand. These jobs require more than a high school education (for example, a short training program to develop the required skill), but often they do not require a college education. In the United States, almost half of the labor force works in these kinds of jobs.

Causes of the Skills Gap

3 Why have we been unable to bridge this gap and prepare workers for the jobs of the future, or even the jobs of today? The answer lies in both the job market and our educational system. The job market is changing more quickly than ever before. Many of the jobs that companies need to fill today did not exist when current job applicants were in school, making it difficult for educational programs to keep up with the demands of the market. Nevertheless, many business leaders argue that schools are not doing enough to provide the technical training that many jobs demand. For example, only a quarter of all schools in the United States teach computer science. Most schools and universities continue to offer the same type of education that they have provided in the past. As a result, many students graduate with degrees that do not prepare them for the jobs that are available. Given this mismatch between the education system and the job market, many labor experts say we cannot and perhaps should not depend on traditional schooling to close the skills gap and should instead find **alternative** solutions.

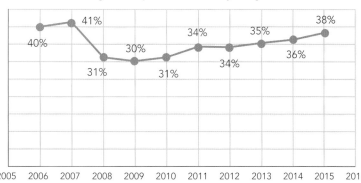

Figure 1
Percentage of Companies with Difficulty Filling Positions

40% 41% 31% 30% 31% 34% 34% 35% 36% 38%

2005 2006 2007 2008 2009 2010 2011 2012 2013 2014 2015 2016

Source: Manpower (2014)

Closing the Skills Gap

4 Both industry and academic experts argue that businesses themselves need to take a more **assertive** role in the preparation of the labor force they require. Businesses have the best information about what skills their employees will need, so it makes sense for them to participate in training **prospective** employees. First, they need to communicate better with schools and universities about the skills they require. Second, they should establish relationships with future employees earlier, perhaps through partnership programs that begin training future employees while they are still students. Finally, businesses may need to develop and provide their own in-house training programs.

5 Technical skills, particularly IT skills, are in high demand, but developing these skills is not necessarily best accomplished by means of a traditional college education. There are a whole range of schools, courses, and training programs that have opened in response to the demand for IT professionals, some in brick-and-mortar classrooms and others online— trade schools[1] for the digital age. The top IT schools are expensive, but some **boast** a 99% placement rate for their graduates, many of whom find positions that pay $100,000 a year or more. Figure 2 displays the predicted job growth in computing jobs.

Figure 2
The Current State of the IT Job Market

1,000,000 more jobs than students by 2020

$500 billion opportunity

1.4 million IT jobs

400,000 computer science students

(y-axis: 200,000 – 1,400,000; x-axis: 2011–2020)

Source: Code.org

6 The skills gap is both **persistent** and expensive. One business expert estimates that a company loses $14,000 when a position remains open for three months. The skills gap is the result of many factors, and there is no single solution to the problems it poses. It is likely that a combination of approaches will be needed before the supply of qualified workers will be able to meet the demand for them.

[1]**trade school** (n) a school where students learn the skills for a job such as electrician, mechanic, or chef

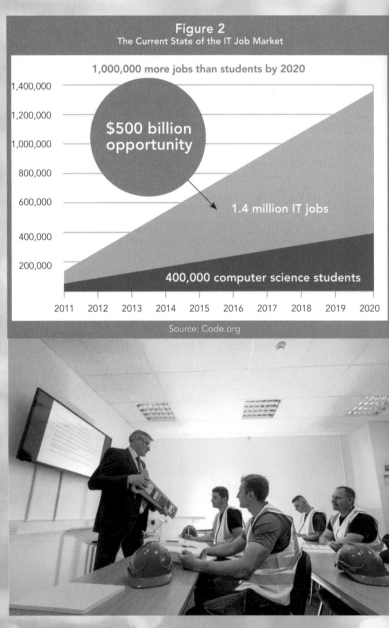

Number of Workers Producing Energy, by Source, 2016

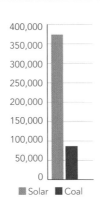

Solar ■ Coal

Job Market Bright for Solar, Dark for Coal

The job picture for U.S. energy workers is rapidly changing. Demand for workers in the once-strong coal industry has fallen off, but prospects have brightened for workers with skills in solar energy. According to a 2017 U.S. Department of Energy report, just under four times as many people were employed in generating electric power from solar sources (373,807 employees) as from coal (86,035 employees).

The U.S. coal industry has shrunk, partly because of concern over environmental damage from mining and burning coal, but also because of economic forces. Coal is costly to extract, ship, and store. As costs have fallen for energy from other sources—especially natural gas, solar, and wind—coal has suffered. There were almost 180,000 coal miners in the U. S. in 1986, a number that fell to only 50,000 in 2016. Coal-rich areas of the U.S. mourn the loss of jobs, which once paid solidly middle-class wages to workers with only high school educations (or less). Wages of $30/hour in 2016 were not unusual. But no amount of pining for old-technology jobs can revive an industry.

The solar industry depends on high-tech devices, but many jobs in the industry, especially for the installers of solar systems, do not require college degrees. And the wages are good (starting at about 75% of what a rookie coal miner would earn). Theoretically, an unemployed coal miner could shift to a job in solar, but that has not often happened. Solar companies require experience—and they require that workers live where the solar-generation facilities are to be installed. Most experienced workers and potential solar sites are not in West Virginia, Kentucky, or other coal regions. Why don't unemployed coal miners move? Mostly because they feel strongly rooted in their hometowns and are reluctant to leave.

Sources:

Federal Reserve Bank of St. Louis (November 3, 2017). FRED: Economic Research, "All Employees, Mining and Logging: Coal Mining. Accessed at https://fred.stlouisfed.org/series/CEU1021210001#0

U.S. Department of Energy (January 2017), U.S. Energy and Employment Report. Accessed at https://energy.gov/sites/prod/files/2017/01/f34/2017%20US%20Energy%20and%20Jobs%20Report_0.pdf

5 READING FOR MAIN IDEAS **Read the report on pages 119–121. Then match the main ideas to each paragraph.**

Main ideas   **Paragraph**

a   Schools that provide training in IT can help fill the skills gap.   _____

b   Employees in the skilled trades and with STEM training are in
    the greatest demand.   _____

c   There is no single solution to the skills gap.   _____

d   Current job applicants do not have the skills that employers are looking for.   _____

e   Businesses need to participate more in preparing future employees.   _____

f   Colleges do not always offer an education with a clear career path.   _____

6 **Which of the statements in Exercise 5 expresses the main idea of the whole text?** _____

7 READING FOR DETAILS **Read the report again. Write *T* (true), *F* (false), or *DNS* (does not say) for each statement below. Correct the false statements.**

_____ 1   Globalization has led to labor shortages in some developing countries.

_____ 2   The most critical labor shortages are in IT fields.

_____ 3   The positions that companies are trying to fill all require a college education.

_____ 4   About 50% of workers in the United States are in the skilled trades.

_____ 5   Most education programs have adapted to meet the new demand for
            technical skills.

_____ 6   Businesses have the most accurate knowledge of the kinds of employees that
            are in demand.

_____ 7   More than 1,000 IT schools and training programs have opened to meet demand.

_____ 8   An unfilled position that remains open for more than three months can cost a
            company about $10,000.

8 ANNOTATING **Make the following annotations in the sidebar on page 121.**

1   Circle the name of the organization that reported the figures about employment in solar
    and coal electrical generation.

2   Underline the three activities in coal-processing that are expensive.

3   Draw a box around the number of people who worked as coal miners in the U.S. in 1986.

4   Highlight the statement of educational qualifications for installers of solar arrays.

READING BETWEEN THE LINES

9 IDENTIFYING PURPOSE AND TONE **Work with a partner. Answer the questions.**

1 What is the purpose of this report?

   a to persuade colleges to change their programs

   b to help job candidates

   c to offer general information

   d to warn employers

2 The author's overall tone in Reading 1 is cautious. Why?

   a Because she is not sure why there is a skills gap.

   b Because it will not be easy to close the skills gap.

   c Because most businesses are not interested in closing the skills gap.

   d Because closing the skills gap may create other problems.

CRITICAL THINKING

10 Work with a partner. Discuss the questions.

UNDERSTAND

What do you think is the $500 billion opportunity in Figure 2?

ANALYZE

Who do you think should take action to improve the skills gap? Why?

EVALUATE

Do you think the trends shown in the graphs will continue in the future? Why or why not?

COLLABORATION

11 A Work in a small group. Do some light research online to learn about the two main visa programs in the United States for skilled workers from other countries, and complete the chart.

type of visa	length of stay in US	kinds of workers allowed
H1B		
H2B		

   B Make a list of at least five advantages and five disadvantages of these programs. Consider the visa holders, their home countries, the employers, American workers, the United States, and the global economy.

   C Share your lists with the class. As a class, decide the five most important pros and cons.

PREPARING TO READ

1 PREDICTING CONTENT USING VISUALS **Work with a partner. You are going to read an article about the value of a college education. Study the graphs in Reading 2 on page 127. Then discuss the questions. After you read the article, come back and check your ideas.**

1 Based on Figure 1, what generalization can you make about college education?

_____

_____

_____

2 Look at Figure 2. What does *median income* mean? Are college-educated workers more likely to earn above or below the median income?

_____

_____

_____

3 What do you think the topic of this article will be? What argument do you think it will make?

_____

_____

_____

2 UNDERSTANDING KEY VOCABULARY **Read the sentences and write the words in bold next to the definitions.**

1 My father suffers from **chronic** pain. He never complains, but I know his back hurts all the time.

2 Steve Jobs was one of the **founders** of Apple, Inc.

3 Business leaders **dispute** the government's claim that the number of jobs has grown.

4 The current protests are an **illustration** of the continuing importance of free speech.

5 There is some **ambiguity** in the law, so it is difficult to know whether the company actually did anything wrong.

6 This new technology has the **potential** to change how students learn about science.

7 The impact of the war on the economy eventually **diminished**, but it took a long time.

8 The consequences of this disaster **extend** beyond the city to the whole country.

a _____ (v) to disagree with

b _____ (n) lack of clarity; the quality of having several possible meanings

c _____ (n) people who establish an organization

d _____ (v) to decrease in size or importance

e _____ (adj) lasting for a long time, especially something bad

f _____ (v) to go further

g _____ (n) the possibility to develop and succeed

h _____ (n) an example that explains something

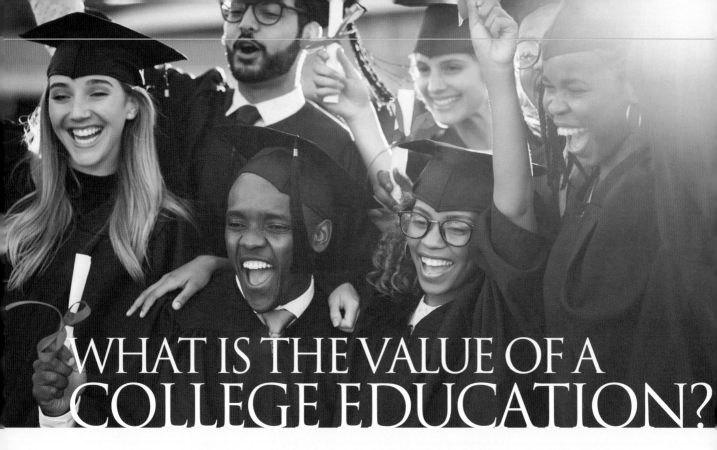

WHAT IS THE VALUE OF A COLLEGE EDUCATION?

1 A college education is a significant investment, so it makes sense to consider carefully whether it is worth the time and money. In good economic times and bad, and in spite of its rising cost, the answer is "yes." According to the Organisation for Economic Cooperation and Development (OECD), around the world the number of people getting a college education is rising steadily (see Figure 1).

The Impact of a College Education

2 A college education has a broad and positive impact. People with a college degree are by far the most likely to enter and remain in the labor force. In OECD countries, average participation in the labor force for those who never completed high school is about 55%. For those with a high school degree, the figure is about 70%, and for college graduates, it is about 83%. College graduates also earn more than those with only a high school degree. In the United States, a new high school graduate earned on average $28,000 per year in 2013, whereas those with a college degree made about $45,000. Over a lifetime, that difference adds up to about a million dollars. Figure 2 provides a dramatic **illustration** of the impact of a college degree on income in selected OECD countries.

3 The consequences of getting—or not getting— a college education **extend** beyond income. There is a strong association between education and health. **Chronic** diseases, such as heart disease and diabetes, pose the greatest risks to public health in developed countries today. These diseases are caused, at least partly, by lifestyle choices, such as poor diet or smoking. In general, people with higher levels of education make healthier lifestyle choices and have greater access to high-quality healthcare.

[1]**Fortune 500 companies** (n) the businesses ranked by *Fortune* magazine as the 500 most profitable companies in the U.S. for a particular year

Income Variance Between Degrees

Figure 1
Percentage of Population (25–64) with a College Education

■ 2000 ■ 2012

Source: OECD Indicators

Figure 2
Percentage of 25–64 Year Olds with a College Degree (2012)

■ At or below the median income
■ More than 2x the median income

Source: OECD Indicators

Figure 1a

■ below OECD average
■ above OECD average

4 It is evident that a college degree provides an economic advantage, but not all degrees have the same earning power. Most analyses suggest that degrees in STEM fields (science, technology, engineering, and math) have the greatest **potential** impact on future income. In the United States, a college graduate with, for example, a chemical engineering degree can expect to earn about $70,000 annually, whereas a graduate with a literature or art degree may be lucky to get $36,000 for an entry-level position. Marc Andreessen, the **founder** of the Internet company Netscape, once declared that someone who studies a non-technical field like literature will probably end up "working in a shoe store."

5 Yet, technical knowledge alone may not be sufficient for success. Steve Jobs, one of the founders of Apple, famously claimed, "It's technology married with liberal arts … that yields the results that make our hearts sing." Other major employers in the technology field agree. Industry leaders say employees from the liberal arts are good at managing **ambiguity**, unlike engineers, who tend to see situations in black and white. Liberal arts graduates can see a problem from multiple perspectives.

6 It is interesting to note that the income gap between liberal arts and STEM graduates gradually **diminishes** as they continue in their careers. In fact, liberal arts degrees are quite common among the world's most highly paid workers. About one-third of the directors of Fortune 500 companies[1] have a liberal arts background. Students, parents, politicians, and industry leaders may argue over which are the most valuable degrees, but the value of a college degree in general cannot be **disputed**.

WHILE READING

3 READING FOR MAIN IDEAS **Read the article on pages 126–127. Write *T* (true), *F* (false), or *DNS* (does not say) for each statement below. Correct the false statements.**

_____ 1 A college education is worth the investment.

_____ 2 College graduates in the U.S. make twice as much as those with just a high school degree.

_____ 3 College graduates generally have healthier lifestyles than those without a college degree.

_____ 4 College graduates are more likely to vote than those without a college degree.

_____ 5 Liberal arts graduates have higher incomes than graduates with an engineering degree.

_____ 6 Liberal arts graduates offer some advantages over graduates with technical degrees.

4 **Read the article again. Which of the statements in Exercise 3 expresses the main idea of the whole text?** _____

5 READING FOR DETAILS **Refer to the graphs in Reading 2 to answer the questions.**

Figure 1

1 Which country had the highest percentage of college graduates in 2012? _____

2 Which country had the largest increase in the percentage of college graduates between 2000 and 2012? _____

3 What percentage of the Mexican population (25–64) had a college degree in 2012? _____

Figure 2

1 Which country had the highest percentage of college graduates with incomes more than twice the median? _____

2 Which country had the highest number of college graduates with incomes at the country median or below? _____

3 What percentage of the college graduates in Brazil earned more than twice the median income? _____

READING BETWEEN THE LINES

6 MAKING INFERENCES **Work with a partner. Discuss the questions.**

1 What relationship, if any, exists among education, income, and health?

2 What do you think Steve Jobs meant by "the results that make our hearts sing"?

3 Based on this excerpt from Reading 2, what are some jobs that liberal arts graduates would be good at? Why?

───────── 66 ─────────

Industry leaders say employees from the liberal arts are good at managing ambiguity, unlike engineers, who tend to see situations in black and white.

⌖ CRITICAL THINKING

7 SYNTHESIZING **Work with a partner. Use ideas from Reading 1 and Reading 2 to discuss the questions.**

APPLY

Why is the impact of a college education on income greater in some countries than in others?

ANALYZE

In your opinion, who should have to study technology? Explain your reasoning.

EVALUATE

Should future income be the primary factor in deciding on a course of study? Why or why not?

COLLABORATION

8 A Work in a small group. Prepare, practice, and perform a role play. Imagine that you are on a TV interview program discussing whether the government should use public money to provide special college scholarships for students in certain high-demand STEM fields.

Roles and positions:

- TV Interviewer - Prepare a list of questions, and interview your guests.
- Expert 1 - You are in favor of these scholarships. Prepare your arguments.
- Expert 2 - You are opposed to these scholarships. Prepare your arguments.

B Practice the interview as a 10-minute TV segment. Record your role play and show it to the class.

COMPLEX NOUN PHRASES

> ### LANGUAGE
>
> English, especially academic English, often uses nouns to modify other nouns. These noun + noun phrases can take many forms:
>
> Compound nouns: healthcare, lifestyle
>
> Separate words: skills gap, stress level
>
> Gerund + noun: parking space, operating costs
>
> There are also noun + noun + noun phrases, but these are less common:
>
> student identification number
>
> application cover letter

1 **Choose one noun from each box to complete the sentences.**

first noun		second noun	
earning	placement	balance	market
entry	training	force	power
job	work–life	level	program
labor		rate	

1 The city community college offers a _____ _____ for people who hope to become airplane mechanics.

2 Statistics clearly demonstrate that a college degree increases lifetime _____ _____ .

3 Our program has an excellent _____ _____ . More than 90% of our graduates find a job within a month.

4 The _____ _____ has been very weak this year, as can be seen from the steady increase in unemployment.

5 The _____ _____ is defined as all the people in the population who are able to work.

6 Recent college graduates usually join a business at the _____ _____ , but some graduates with a STEM background are able to find higher-level positions.

7 Salary is an important consideration in choosing a career, but a career that offers a good _____ _____ is just as important.

2 **Unscramble the words to create complex noun phrases. Then use them correctly in the sentences below.**

a   information / professional / technology   _____

b   training / graduate / program   _____

c   participation / rate / force / labor   _____

d   enrollment / trends / college   _____

e   household / income / median   _____

1   The _____ in the United States is just over $50,000 per year.

2   A local car parts factory announced that it will hire its first
    _____ this summer.

3   If you want a secure future, you may want to consider a career as a(n)
    _____ .

4   The _____ in the United States has fluctuated between
    60% and 70% in the past ten years.

5   The U.S. Department of Education keeps track of _____
    and reports its data every year.

WATCH AND LISTEN

GLOSSARY

second shift (n) a work period that usually begins in the late afternoon and ends in the late evening (such as in a factory or hospital)

welder (n) a person whose job is joining metal parts together with high heat

hydrogen (n) the lightest gas, one of the chemical elements

instrument technician (n) a worker trained to operate specialized machines or equipment

vocational education (also known as career and technical education) (n) schooling where students learn skills that involve working with their hands

PREPARING TO WATCH

1 ACTIVATING YOUR KNOWLEDGE **Work with a partner. Discuss the questions.**

1 Are you familiar with any specialized high schools? How is their curriculum different from a traditional high school? How might a specialized high school benefit students?

2 What do most young people do after completing high school?

3 What job opportunities exist for young people after high school?

2 PREDICTING CONTENT USING VISUALS **Look at the images from the video. Answer both questions for each one.**

1 What job does this person have?

2 What kind of training is needed for this job?

WHILE WATCHING

 **3** UNDERSTANDING MAIN IDEAS **Watch the video. Check (✓) the ideas you hear.**

1 Nick had more than one job offer when he graduated from a career and technical high school. ☐

2 Air Products manufactures high-tech equipment. ☐

3 John McGlade has to train the skilled workers he needs. ☐

4 Government support for vocational education is decreasing. ☐

5 Not many young people are interested in vocational education. ☐

4 UNDERSTANDING DETAILS **Watch the video again. Write a detail for each main idea.**

1 Air Products has 7,500 workers, and not all are skilled.

_____

2 John McGlade's company often has positions available.

_____

3 Career and technical education has been cut, and more cuts may be on the way.

_____

4 Vocational schools train students to work in technical careers.

_____

☼ CRITICAL THINKING

5 **Work with a partner. Discuss the questions.**

APPLY	ANALYZE	EVALUATE
Would you have been interested in attending a career and technical high school? Why or why not?	What kind of a person is a good candidate for a career and technical high school? Explain your reasoning.	What are the advantages and disadvantages of entering the workforce shortly after high school?

🗑 COLLABORATION

6 **A** Work in a small group. Study the pie chart. It shows the factors used by *U.S. News and World Report* to evaluate the 100 best jobs each year.

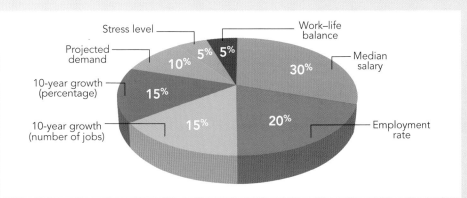

B Discuss the criteria. Do you agree about the relative importance of these factors? If not, which factors would you rate the most highly?

C Make a pie chart that reflects your priorities and present it to the class.

HEALTH SCIENCES

Key Reading Skill	Recognizing discourse organization
Additional Reading Skills	Using your knowledge; understanding key vocabulary; reading for main ideas; taking notes; making inferences; scanning to predict content; reading for details; synthesizing
Language Development	Verbs and verb phrases for causation; health and medicine word families

ACTIVATE YOUR KNOWLEDGE

Work with a partner. Discuss the questions.

1   What do you think is happening in this photo?

2   Which diseases do you think are the greatest threats to global health today?

3   Do you think the world's population is healthier now than a hundred years ago? Why or why not?

4   The world's population is more interconnected than ever before. What effect do you think this has on global health?

READING 1

PREPARING TO READ

1 USING YOUR KNOWLEDGE **You are going to read an article about superbugs. Work with a partner. Discuss the questions.**

1   When you are feeling sick and go to a doctor's office or clinic, do you usually get antibiotics? Why or why not?

2   Do you always finish all the medication the doctor prescribes even if you are feeling better? Why or why not?

3   Why do you think antibiotics are commonly given to livestock, that is, animals that produce food for humans?

2 UNDERSTANDING KEY VOCABULARY **Read the sentences and choose the best definition for each vocabulary item in bold.**

1   The Internet has **revolutionized** almost everything we do, from shopping to studying.

   a   made easier

   b   completely changed

   c   made more accessible

2   The news report presented a **grim** picture of the life and experiences of the war refugees.

   a   very bad; worrisome

   b   dangerous

   c   conflicting; unclear

3   Mosquitoes **thrive** in warm, wet conditions, so they are more common in summer.

   a   live and develop successfully

   b   compete with each other more easily

   c   struggle to survive

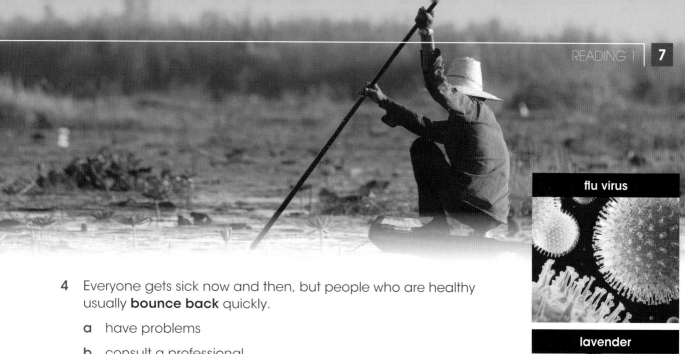

flu virus

4 Everyone gets sick now and then, but people who are healthy usually **bounce back** quickly.

   a have problems

   b consult a professional

   c return to normal

lavender

5 Business **cycles** involve periods of economic expansion, followed by downturns, and then periods of expansion again.

   a office environments

   b publications

   c repeating series of events

6 Scientists have discovered that some common plants have **therapeutic** properties. Chemicals from the plants are beneficial to patients with a variety of conditions.

   a economic

   b substantial

   c healing

Asian tiger mosquito

7 City workers are spraying chemicals in wet areas to **counter** the recent increase in the mosquito population. City officials worry that these insects may spread diseases.

   a defend against

   b investigate

   c keep track of

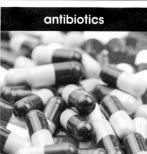

antibiotics

8 He had a very **mild** case of the flu, so he was able to go back to work after only a few days.

   a not contagious

   b not extreme

   c not pleasant

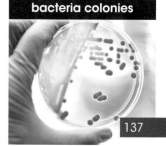

bacteria colonies

SUPERBUGS

1 They are so small that you need a microscope to see them, but so powerful that they kill an average of 37,000 people in the United States every year. They are superbugs—drug-resistant bacteria that have emerged since antibiotics **revolutionized** medicine in the early 20th century. Indeed, the rise of these superbugs and the use of antibiotics are closely intertwined.

2 All organisms change over time; this is a basic principle of evolution. Smaller organisms, such as bacteria, are able to evolve more quickly, adapting as circumstances require. In the face of antibiotics, bacteria have adapted with deadly efficiency. When a patient takes antibiotics to fight off a bacterial infection, the goal is to kill the bacteria causing the infection. Often, however, although most of the bacteria are killed, a few of the strongest bacteria survive. Thus, only these drug-resistant bacteria are able to reproduce. This sets up a **cycle** in which increasingly powerful antibiotics are needed to **counter** bacterial infections, eventually resulting in the development of superbugs—bacteria able to resist even the most powerful drugs.

3 Scientists believe that a large part of this cycle is preventable. Few would dispute that patients who are genuinely ill should take antibiotics, but one recent study suggested that almost 50% of all antibiotic use is inappropriate or unnecessary. Some patients take antibiotics for ailments that would eventually clear up on their own, or for viral infections, against which antibiotics have no effect. In addition, some patients do not finish their course of medication, allowing bacteria to **bounce back**, but stronger. All of these factors contribute to the rise and spread of superbugs. Although many doctors find it difficult to refuse when patients request medication, in this instance, what may be safe and effective for the individual can be harmful to society as a whole.

4 Another major factor that promotes the spread of drug resistance is the use of antibiotics for livestock. The Natural Resources Defense Council reports that 80% of antibiotic use in the United States is for animals. In part, the drugs are used to prevent the spread of infection among animals, especially those that live in crowded conditions. However, farmers also use antibiotics because these drugs help animals to gain weight quickly. Unfortunately, such non-**therapeutic** use of antibiotics is problematic because it kills off the beneficial bacteria that normally live in the animals' digestive tract, leaving drug-resistant strains of bacteria to **thrive**.

5 The widespread use of antibiotics for the past 70 years in both the animal and human populations, and the resulting increase in drug-resistant bacteria, have fueled an ongoing search for more powerful drugs. In the early days of antibiotic research, scientists were successful in finding new classes of drugs, capable of fighting the drug-resistant bacteria that continually appeared. Since then, however, drug discovery has tapered off to almost nothing (see Figure 1). Very few weapons remain against the deadliest bacteria. Late in 2015, researchers reported the emergence of a strain of bacteria able to resist even the most powerful medications, those only used as a last resort.

6 What can be done to stop this cycle? Scientists maintain that as individuals, we can make a difference with simple steps, such as regular hand washing. It is also important that patients understand that antibiotics are not always the right course of treatment. They should not be taken for viral infections or even for **mild** bacterial infections. Finally, it is crucial to take antibiotics out of the food chain. Fortunately, consumers are pushing for this, so we are likely to see changes in this practice in the near future. The fast food giant McDonald's, which sells millions of pounds of chicken every year, has begun using only antibiotic-free chicken. If both individuals and corporations around the world continue to take steps like these, perhaps superbugs can be stopped. The alternative presents a **grim** picture for future generations.

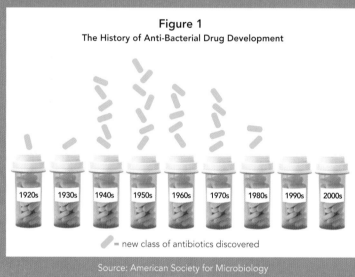

Figure 1
The History of Anti-Bacterial Drug Development

| 1920s | 1930s | 1940s | 1950s | 1960s | 1970s | 1980s | 1990s | 2000s |

= new class of antibiotics discovered

Source: American Society for Microbiology

3 READING FOR MAIN IDEAS **Read the article on pages 138–139. Which of these statements best expresses the main idea of the article?**

a Bacteria will always find a way to get around antibiotics.

b Antibiotics in the food chain have led to the spread of drug-resistant bacteria.

c The misuse of antibiotics is a primary factor in the rise of drug-resistant bacteria.

d Since our strongest antibiotics are powerless against the latest strain of bacteria, we should expect more outbreaks of dangerous diseases.

🛠 SKILLS

RECOGNIZING DISCOURSE ORGANIZATION

Essays are usually organized to meet general goals. An essay may

- describe a process
- compare and/or contrast two or more things
- describe the causes or consequences of things
- explain how something works
- describe a system of classification
- relate a series of events

Recognizing these discourse patterns can help you predict and comprehend the content of a text.

---

4 RECOGNIZING DISCOURSE ORGANIZATION **Which discourse pattern best describes Reading 1?**

_____

5 TAKING NOTES **Read the article again. Complete the events in the causal chain of drug resistance.**

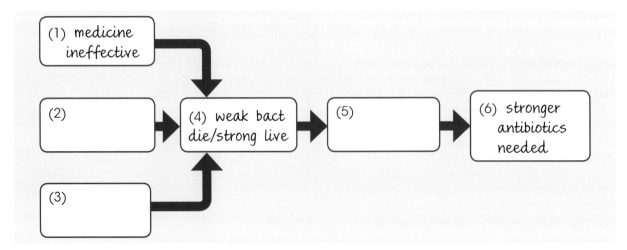

(1) medicine ineffective

(2)

(3)

(4) weak bact die/strong live

(5)

(6) stronger antibiotics needed

READING BETWEEN THE LINES

6 MAKING INFERENCES **Find these phrases in Reading 1. Try to infer their meaning from context and match them to the correct definition below.**

1 closely intertwined (para 1)   **a** without help

2 in the face of (para 2)   **b** connected; difficult to separate

3 on their own (para 3)   **c** gradually become weaker or happen less often

4 taper off (para 5)   **d** when every other option has failed

5 as a last resort (para 5)   **e** when threatened by

7 **Work with a partner. Write a sentence for each phrase in Exercise 6, using the phrase in context correctly. Share your sentences with the class.**

⌁ CRITICAL THINKING

8 **Work with a partner. Discuss the questions.**

APPLY

What does Figure 1 in Reading 1 show? What do you think will happen in the future?

ANALYZE

Do you think farmers should give healthy animals antibiotics to prevent disease? Why or why not?

EVALUATE

Should patients be able to demand medication from a doctor if it may or may not help?

⚇ COLLABORATION

9 **A** Work in a small group. Research the superbug called Methicillin-resistant Staphylococcus aureus (MRSA). Answer the questions.

- Why is MRSA an especially troubling infection?
- How do people become infected?
- What physical damage can it do to a person?
- What treatments can fight it?

B Create a poster or slideshow that expresses your findings about MRSA. Include visuals such as diagrams of how MRSA infection happens, maps of where MRSA is most common, pictures showing MRSA symptoms, etc. Show and explain your poster or slideshow to the class.

PREPARING TO READ

1 SCANNING TO PREDICT CONTENT **You are going to read an article about infection. Scan the article and the maps on pages 144–146 to answer these questions.**

1 What is *Aedes aegypti*? _____

_____

2 What does it do? _____

_____

3 What does the first map show? _____

_____

4 How does the U.S. habitat of *Aedes aegypti* differ from that of *Aedes albopictus*?

_____

_____

5 What do you think you will learn about in this article?

_____

_____

2 UNDERSTANDING KEY VOCABULARY **Read the sentences and write the words in bold next to the definitions.**

1   The new housing development's **proximity** to the airport is a problem because of the noise.

2   The military uses a secret code for the **transmission** of messages from headquarters to soldiers in the field.

3   The damage from the fire was **confined** to the third and fourth floors of the building.

4   It is not possible to **eradicate** some diseases, but it is possible to control them.

5   Social media sites **facilitate** the sharing of information. News can spread around the globe in an instant.

6   Early **detection** of cancer can substantially improve the chances of recovery.

7   There has been a **surge** in complaints about dangerous chemicals in the drinking water since farm animals started mysteriously dying.

8   Many rural populations depend on **domesticated** animals for food and labor.

a   _____ (n) the notice or discovery of something

b   _____ (n) nearness

c   _____ (n) a sudden, large increase

d   _____ (v) to make something possible or easier

e   _____ (n) the process of passing something from one person or place to another

f   _____ (v) to exist in or apply to a limited group or area

g   _____ (adj) under human control; used for animals

h   _____ (v) to get rid of something completely

THE GLOBALIZATION OF INFECTION

1 Recent headlines have been filled with alarming news of the spread of pathogens[1] that cause diseases like SARS, MERS, swine flu, dengue fever, chikungunya, and the latest—the Zika virus. Are these pathogens really on the increase, or have **detection** and reporting methods simply improved? In fact, several studies suggest that the **surge** in these infectious diseases is quite real. Researchers propose a number of reasons for these developments.

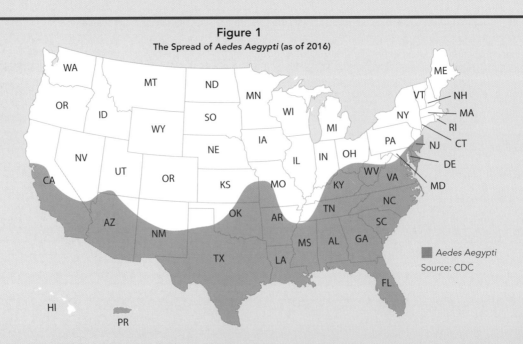

Figure 1
The Spread of *Aedes Aegypti* (as of 2016)

■ *Aedes Aegypti*
Source: CDC

2 Probably the most obvious reason is how closely connected the world has become. Human populations regularly travel long distances as immigrants, business travelers, or tourists, carrying diseases with them. For example, it is thought that the Zika virus may have traveled from French Polynesia to Brazil in the blood of infected international athletes. People are not the only world travelers; insects, primarily mosquitoes, can also hop on a boat or a plane and migrate thousands of miles. Scientists refer to the hosts that carry pathogens as *vectors*. When they bite, vectors transfer infected blood to a new victim, spreading the pathogen in both humans and animal populations. As these vectors move around the world, and if they can survive and reproduce in their new environment, the range of the disease grows.

[1]**pathogen** (n) a small organism that can cause disease
[2]**mutate** (v) to change genetically

3 The pathogens themselves are also highly adaptable. Most pathogens are found in a specific vector. For example, chikungunya is carried by a particular type of mosquito, *Aedes aegypti*, in Africa and Asia, where the disease originated. As the virus traveled across the Pacific, however, it mutated[2] to a new form, which thrives in a different vector, the Asian tiger mosquito, *Aedes albopictus*, allowing the disease to spread beyond the habitat of the original host mosquito.

4 Many infectious diseases originated in warm climates, where insects like mosquitoes live and thrive. As climate change leads to higher temperatures around the world, mosquitoes are now able to survive in areas that were once too cold for them. Figure 1 shows the range of *Aedes albopictus* and *Aedes aegypti*, both major vectors of tropical diseases, in the United States as of 2016. *Aedes aegypti*, once **confined** to tropical Africa, is expected to expand its range even farther with global warming.

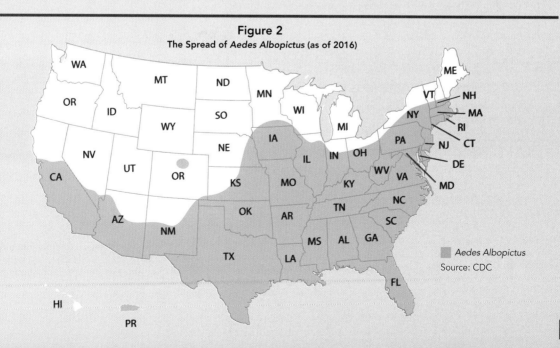

Figure 2
The Spread of *Aedes Albopictus* (as of 2016)

Aedes Albopictus
Source: CDC

5 The increasingly urban nature of the world's population also **facilitates** the **transmission** of disease. In large, crowded cities in developing countries, many people do not have regular household waste collection or access to clean drinking water. A household without running water is likely to catch and save rainwater in open containers, the perfect breeding ground[3] for mosquitoes, as are piles of trash and, above all, old tires.

6 Another aspect of urbanization contributing to the spread of pathogens is our close **proximity** to both wild and **domesticated** animals. Many dangerous pathogens have the ability to mutate and jump from one species to another, including to humans. Avian and swine flu are prime examples of such cross-species transfer, as is Ebola, which scientists believe originated among gorillas and chimpanzees. As various species experience the destruction of their habitats as a result of deforestation and urbanization, many are forced to live closer to human settlements, increasing the opportunity for the transmission of diseases from animals to humans. Domesticated animal populations are being squeezed as well. They are confined to increasingly crowded spaces, creating conditions that facilitate the transmission of disease.

7 Some pathogens, such as the ones that cause Ebola, are deadly, with no known cure. Others may not be as dangerous but still have an enormous economic impact in terms of lost productivity and the resources needed to fight them and provide healthcare for their victims. Some of these infectious diseases, once a local menace, now pose a global threat, and it will require a global effort to **eradicate** them.

[3]**breeding ground** (n) a place where organisms reproduce

> ## Avian and swine flu are prime examples of such cross-species transfer

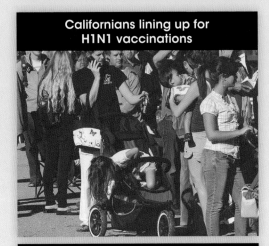

Californians lining up for H1N1 vaccinations

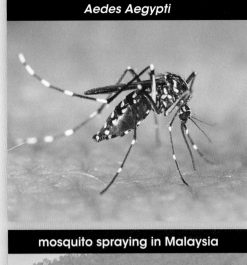

Aedes Aegypti

mosquito spraying in Malaysia

WHILE READING

3 READING FOR MAIN IDEAS **Read the article. Which statement do you think the writer of the article would agree with?**

a Infectious diseases are a concern for people all over the world.

b Scientists will soon find ways to prevent and treat these diseases.

c Slowing global warming is the key to eradicating these diseases.

d Most of these diseases are not likely to pose a threat to the United States in the near future.

4 READING FOR DETAILS **Read the article again. Check (✓) the factors that contribute to the spread of infectious diseases as discussed in the article. Find four other factors that were discussed in the article and add them to the list.**

a climate change ☐

b mutation of pathogens ☐

c lack of access to healthcare ☐

d global movement of populations ☐

e drug resistance ☐

f migration of vectors ☐

g floods ☐

(1) _____

(2) _____

(3) _____

(4) _____

5 **Use the phrases from the boxes to label the causal chains that start with urbanization.**

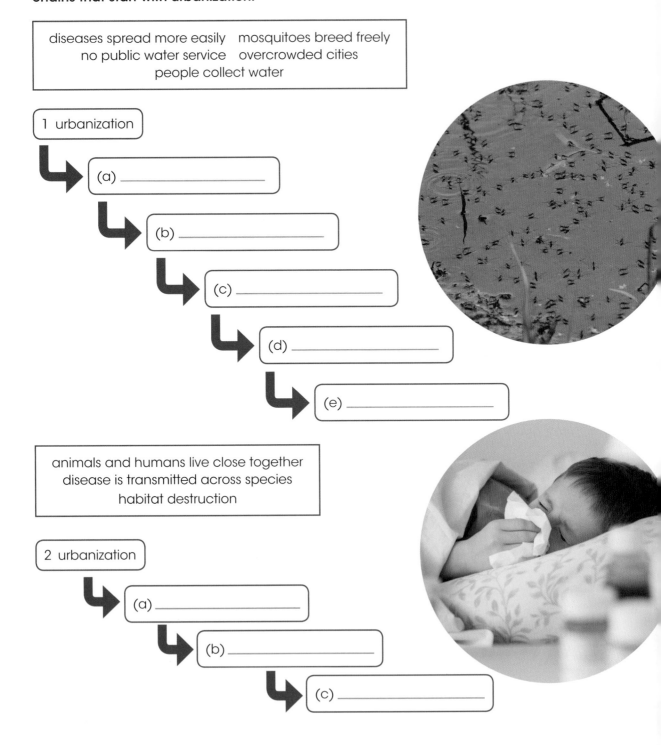

diseases spread more easily	mosquitoes breed freely
no public water service	overcrowded cities
	people collect water

1 urbanization

(a) _____

(b) _____

(c) _____

(d) _____

(e) _____

| animals and humans live close together |
| disease is transmitted across species |
| habitat destruction |

2 urbanization

(a) _____

(b) _____

(c) _____

READING BETWEEN THE LINES

6 MAKING INFERENCES **Work with a partner. Discuss the questions.**

1 In paragraph 6, the writer says that clean water and garbage collection are not available to some people, which implies that they are available to others. Who do you think gets these services? Why?

2 Is the writer optimistic or pessimistic about the future spread of pathogens? How do you know?

☀ CRITICAL THINKING

7 SYNTHESIZING **Work with a partner. Use ideas from Reading 1 and Reading 2 to discuss the questions.**

APPLY

Both articles end by saying a global effort will be required to combat the spread of pathogens. What do you think can be done?

EVALUATE

Antibiotics are for bacterial infections, but they are sometimes part of a larger treatment plan for viral diseases. What effect might this have on the increase in superbugs?

COLLABORATION

8 A Work in a small group. Read the case history of dengue fever in the table.

	dengue fever
First reported	17th century
Geographic range	worldwide
Annual infections	50–100 million
Annual fatalities	22,000
Vectors	*Aedes aegypti* and *Aedes albopictus*
Conditions for transmission	crowded conditions needed to sustain transmission among humans
Vaccine	in development
Treatment	no specific treatment

B Choose one of the following infectious diseases or another one that interests you.

- Ebola
- influenza
- Lyme disease
- Q fever
- trichinosis
- Zika

Do research on the disease you chose. Create a new table with the information you find.

C Compare your table with another group.

VERBS AND VERB PHRASES FOR CAUSATION

LANGUAGE

In order to read and write with precision, it is important to understand the differences in meaning among verbs and verb phrases that express aspects of causation.

Direct causation

Many diseases, such as malaria and chikungunya, **result from** the bite of a mosquito carrying the pathogen.

Makes effect easier to achieve

The poverty and crowded conditions in many modern cities **facilitate** the transmission of infectious diseases.

Part of a cause

Climate change **has contributed** to the spread of tropical diseases.

Passive causation

Global travel **allows** pathogens to spread more easily.

direct causation	part of cause	makes effect easier to achieve	passive causation
cause / be a cause of lead to result in be a/the result of create trigger produce bring about drive	be a factor contribute to affect impact influence have an effect on have a role in	help facilitate promote fuel encourage foster enable	let* allow permit

* Notice that, unlike other passive causation verbs, *let* is not followed by *to*:
*Global travel **lets** pathogens **spread** more easily.*

1 **Complete the sentences with one of the verbs or verb phrases from the chart above. More than one answer is possible.**

1 Health experts emphasize the importance of human behavior because our decisions can both _____ and prevent the spread of antibiotic-resistant superbugs.

2 Scientists have only recently begun to understand how climate change _____ the spread of vectors that carry infectious diseases.

3 Health officials are targeting containers of standing water that _____ mosquitoes to reproduce and spread disease.

4 A bacterial infection _____ an automatic response in which the body attempts to kill off the invading pathogens

5 Antibiotics often destroy only a percentage of the bacteria that cause infection, _____ the strongest to survive and even thrive.

2 Write two more sentences using expressions from the chart on page 150.

1 _____

_____

2 _____

_____

HEALTH AND MEDICINE WORD FAMILIES

3 Complete the word families related to global health and medicine.
Use a dictionary to help you if needed.

noun	verb	adjective	
access	(1) _____	(2) _____	
bacteria		(3) _____	
(4) _____	(5) _____	infectious	
(6) _____	mutate	mutant	
prevention	(7) _____	(8) _____	(9) _____
(10) _____	(11) _____	resistant	
therapy		(12) _____	
transmission	(13) _____	(14) _____	(15) _____
virus		(16) _____	

4 Complete the paragraph with words from Exercise 3 in the correct form.

The spread of infectious disease is a complex phenomenon. Health officials must deal with both (1)_____ and (2)_____ infections, caused by pathogens that can be (3)_____ from one host to another in different ways. What makes the situation even more challenging is that these pathogens can (4)_____ over time, allowing them to become (5)_____ to medications. Once this occurs, these drugs are no longer (6)_____ , and scientists need to find new ways to treat the infections. Many experts believe that a better option would be to develop a vaccine to (7)_____ these diseases from (8)_____ people in the first place.

WATCH AND LISTEN

GLOSSARY

agonizing (adj)   causing extreme physical or mental pain

E. coli (n)   a type of bacteria that lives in the intestines of humans and other animals, and causes severe illness

contaminate (v)   to make something less pure or make it toxic

mutation (n)   a change that happens in an organism's genes that can be passed to new organisms by reproduction, or the process of this change

lethal strain (n)   a deadly virus that is only slightly different from other viruses of the same type

skyrocket (v)   to rise extremely quickly

PREPARING TO WATCH

1 ACTIVATING YOUR KNOWLEDGE   **Work with a partner. Discuss the questions.**

1   Have you ever gotten really sick from something you ate? What type of food was it? How long were you sick?

2   What types of food are more likely to cause illness?

3   What steps do you take to prevent food poisoning and other food-related illnesses?

2 PREDICTING CONTENT USING VISUALS   **Look at the pictures from the video. Discuss the questions with your partner.**

1   What do you think is being studied or researched?

2   Are you familiar with the CDC (Centers for Disease Control and Prevention)? What do you think their role is?

3   Who develops new treatments or medicines? How long do you think it takes to develop new medicines?

WHILE WATCHING

▶ **3** UNDERSTANDING MAIN IDEAS   **Watch the video. Write *T* (true) or *F* (false) next to the statements. Correct the false statements.**

____ 1   Tom Dukes had emergency surgery due to an *E. coli* virus infection.

____ 2   Superbugs develop genes that are resistant to current antibiotics.

_____ **3** Antibiotics are often unnecessarily prescribed.

_____ **4** Pharmaceutical companies can develop new drugs in a short amount
of time.

(▶) **4** UNDERSTANDING DETAILS **Watch the video again. Complete each sentence.**

1 Before contracting *E. coli* from contaminated meat, Tom Dukes …

_____

2 According to Dr. Spellberg, drug-resistant superbugs begin as …

_____

3 A recent study documented an overuse of antibiotics, noting that …

_____

4 Drug companies are investing more money into the drugs …

_____

✦ CRITICAL THINKING

5 **Work with a partner. Discuss the questions.**

APPLY	ANALYZE	EVALUATE
Why does it take so long and cost so much money to develop a new antibiotic?	What do you think are the reasons antibiotics are overprescribed?	Do you think the emergence of drug-resistant bacteria is a public health crisis? Why or why not?

COLLABORATION

6 **A** Work in a small group. Imagine you are members of a task force in the World Health
Organization (WHO) and must develop an international strategy for cooperatively
fighting superbugs. Think about:

- current international health programs
- the policies of individual nations
- how to influence governments
- organizations to work with
- sources of funding

B Write a one-page, detailed, concise strategy. Include specific steps as short
bullet points.

C Present and explain your strategy to the class. Include time for Q & A.

COLLABORATION

LEARNING OBJECTIVES

Key Reading Skill	Using context clues to understand terminology and fixed expressions
Additional Reading Skills	Understanding key vocabulary; previewing; reading for main ideas; summarizing; reading for details; working out meaning; using your knowledge; taking notes
Language Development	Language for hedging

ACTIVATE YOUR KNOWLEDGE

Work with a partner. Discuss the questions.

1   Do you prefer to play team sports or individual sports? Which do you prefer to watch? Why?

2   Which is more productive—when members of a group compete or collaborate? Explain your answer.

3   Do you agree or disagree with the following statement? Give reasons for your answer.

   A team's goals are more important than the goals of its individual members.

1 UNDERSTANDING KEY VOCABULARY **Read the definitions. Complete the sentences with the correct form of each vocabulary item in bold.**

---

accomplish (v)   to do something successfully

coordinate (v)   to make separate things or people work well together

decline (v)   to worsen; to decrease

detract from (v)   to make something worse or less valuable

differentiate (v)   to show or find the difference between one thing and another

enhance (v)   to improve

isolate (v)   to separate something from other connected things

phenomenon (n)   something that can be experienced or felt, especially something that is unusual or new

---

1   The soft colors and elegant furniture _____ the restaurant's appearance.

2   We can't work independently. We'll need to _____ our efforts if we want this project to be a success.

3   Sales have _____ since the government increased taxes on consumer goods.

4   We have _____ a lot in the last five years, but we still have more work to do in order to reach our goals.

5   El Niño is a _____ that brings unpredictable and unusual weather to many parts of the world.

6   The bright colors of the male bird's feathers _____ it from the female.

7   Cans, bottles, and other garbage _____ the natural beauty of the beach.

8   Doctors have been unable to _____ the cause of the patient's fever, so they are doing more tests.

2 PREVIEWING You are going to read an article about the value of talented individuals within teams. Work with a partner. Read the first sentence of each paragraph in the article on pages 158–159. Discuss the questions and write short answers.

1 What broader lessons do you think we can learn from sports teams?

_____

_____

2 What do you think chickens have to do with sports?

_____

_____

3 How important is the talent of individual players to a team's success?

_____

_____

Chickens establish a pecking order.

THE VALUE OF TALENT

1 Much of the work in today's world is **accomplished** in teams: in business, in scientific research, in government, on movie sets, and of course, in sports. Most people believe that the best way to build a great team is to assemble a group of the best, most talented individuals. Facebook's Mark Zuckerberg, commenting on the value of talent, is quoted as saying that one great engineer is worth a hundred average ones. And Zuckerberg is certainly someone who knows how to build an A-team.

2 Animal scientist William Muir wondered if he could build such an A-team—with chickens. He looked for the most productive egg producers and bred[1] them for six generations. This was his test group. For comparison, he did the same thing with a selection of average egg producers. This was his control group. To his surprise, six generations later, he found that the egg production of the test group was lower than that of the control group. He discovered that the super-producers in the test group used an enormous amount of energy constantly re-establishing a pecking order, keeping themselves at the top. As a result, they had little energy left for egg production.

3 Of course, chickens are not a team, but this kind of group interaction and its effect on production piqued the interest of researchers who study teams and teamwork. The owners of sports teams spend millions of dollars to attract top talent[2]. Companies spend millions to hire top businesspeople. They want to know if their money is well spent.

4 A recent series of studies examined the role of talent in the sports world. They focused on three different sports: World Cup soccer, professional basketball, and professional baseball. The results were mixed. For soccer and basketball, the studies revealed that adding talented players to a team is indeed a good strategy, but only up to a point. Performance peaked when about 70% of the players were considered top talent; above that level, the team's performance began to **decline**. Interestingly, this trend was not evident in baseball, where additional individual talent continued to **enhance** the team's performance (Figures 1 and 2).

5 In looking for an explanation for the different results for different sports, the researchers **isolated** one important factor—the extent to which a good performance by a team requires its members to **coordinate** their actions. This task interdependence **differentiates** baseball from basketball and soccer. In baseball, the performance of individual players is less dependent on teammates than in soccer and basketball. The researchers concluded that when, during the course of play, task interdependence is high, team performance will suffer when there is too much talent in the group. When task interdependence is lower, on the other hand, individual talent will have a positive effect on team performance.

[1]**bred** (v; past and past participle of breed) for animals and plants, managed and controlled the reproduction of

[2]**talent** (n) especially in sports and entertainment, a collective term for the people possessing notable talent

Figure 1
Team Performance as a Function of Top Talent on the Team: World Cup Soccer

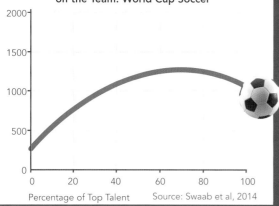

Team Performance

Percentage of Top Talent

Source: Swaab et al, 2014

Figure 2
Team Performance as a Function of Top Talent on the Team: Major League Baseball

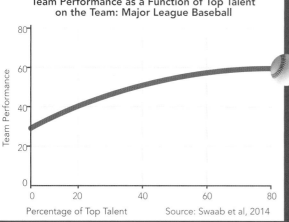

Team Performance

Percentage of Top Talent

Source: Swaab et al, 2014

6 One explanation for this **phenomenon** is not so far from the pecking order situation among chickens. If a basketball star is pursuing his own personal goals, for example, trying to amass a high personal point total, he may be less generous as a team player. He may take a shot himself when it would be better to pass the ball to a teammate, **detracting from** the team's overall performance. Young children learning to play team sports are often told, "There is no *I* in *TEAM*." Stars apparently do not follow this basic principle of sportsmanship.

7 Another possibility is that when there is a lot of talent on a team, some players may begin to make less effort. This is referred to as the *Ringelmann effect*. Maximilien Ringelmann, a French agricultural engineer, conducted an experiment in 1913 in which he asked two, three, four, and up to 28 people to participate in a game of tug-of-war. He measured how much force each person used to pull the rope. He found that whenever he added a person to the team, everyone else pulled with less force.

8 Assembling the ideal team—for sports, business, science, or entertainment—is more complicated than simply hiring the best talent. An A-team may require a balance—not just A players, but a few generous B players as well.

3 READING FOR MAIN IDEAS **Read the article on pages 158–159. Highlight the sentences that express the main ideas. Highlight only key points—no more than five sentences.**

4 SUMMARIZING **Complete the summary. Then compare your work with a partner.**

> Some sports teams are a lot like chickens. Too many high-level individual performers
> (1)_____ from the (2)_____ of the group. This is most likely to happen
> in sports such as soccer and (3)_____ , in which team members need to
> (4)_____ their actions. Star athletes, like star chickens, may be more likely to
> (5)_____ their own goals than work for the group's best interests.

5 READING FOR DETAILS **Scan the article to find these terms. Explain them in your own words.**

a   task interdependence

b   the Ringelmann effect

READING BETWEEN THE LINES

⚒ SKILLS

USING CONTEXT CLUES TO UNDERSTAND TERMINOLOGY

Formal writing often contains topic-specific terminology and expressions as well as higher-level vocabulary that readers may not know. Elements of context can help you determine the meaning of unfamiliar terms. Here are some context clues to look for.

Cultural or world knowledge

*Before the games, athletes carry the Olympic **torch** to cities around the host country.*

Everyone is familiar with the tradition of athletes carrying the symbol of the Games, the Olympic flame, so you can guess the meaning of *torch*.

Components of multiword expressions or parts of words

*Recent trade figures are evidence of the **interdependence** of the two countries.*

You already know the meaning of the two parts, *inter + dependence*, so you can guess the meaning of the term.

Contrast

*The committee rejected the job candidate. He didn't seem very energetic, and they were looking for someone more **dynamic**.*

So someone who is dynamic is the opposite of someone with low energy.

SKILLS

USING CONTEXT CLUES TO UNDERSTAND TERMINOLOGY (CONT.)

Examples

Typhoons, such as the devastating storm Haiyan in the Philippines in 2013, can cause considerable damage.

If you are familiar with the storm named Haiyan, you can guess the meaning of *typhoon*.

Logical inference

Scientists **bred** chickens for six generations to examine their behavior over time.

If you consider what scientists could do to chickens for six generations with the purpose of understanding their behavior, you can guess the meaning of *bred*.

6 WORKING OUT MEANING   **Work with a partner. Use context clues to discuss the possible meaning of these terms from Reading 1.**

1 **A-team** (paragraph 1): What does the term mean? Is it limited to sports?

2 **pecking order** (paragraph 2): Chickens peck one another to show dominance. How could this relate to teams in different contexts?

3 **tug-of-war** (paragraph 7): Read the paragraph and describe what you think happens in this game. Do an image search to check your ideas. How might this term be used in other contexts?

CRITICAL THINKING

7 **Work with a partner. Discuss the questions.**

APPLY

Describe a personal experience of working in a group (music group, class project, volunteering, etc.)

ANALYZE

What factors do you think contributed to the group's success or lack of success?

EVALUATE

Was it a positive or negative experience? Explain your reasoning.

COLLABORATION

8 A Work in a small group. Prepare a short humorous sketch about how NOT to do group work. First, brainstorm factors that cause group work to be ineffective. Next, think of some situations that have resulted when group work goes wrong. Finally, choose three or four situations to act out as short scenes in your sketch.

B Divide the roles for your sketch. One person will be the narrator who explains the scenes. The other members of your group will be actors.

C Write a script and practice it. Your sketch should be no more than 10 minutes long. Act out your sketch for the class.

READING 2

1 USING YOUR KNOWLEDGE **You are going to read an article about group intelligence. Do you think each statement is true (T) or false (F)?**

_____ 1 The intelligence of a group is equal to the intelligence of its members added together.

_____ 2 People who have similar interests and backgrounds work together better than people who are very different.

_____ 3 You can tell a lot about how well people are communicating by just looking at their facial expressions.

_____ 4 Communication works best when people believe that others will respect what they say.

_____ 5 In a meeting, it is a waste of time for people to talk to each other instead of listening to the leader.

_____ 6 People can communicate just as effectively using technology (IM, email, teleconferencing) as they can meeting face to face.

2 **After you have finished reading the article, check your answers to Exercise 1.**

Bees are nature's most efficient builders.

3 UNDERSTANDING KEY VOCABULARY **Read the sentences and write the words in bold next to the definitions.**

1 He held his fists high in the air, a **gesture** that made it very clear how excited he was.

2 If you want to be well prepared for the test, you should study in a quiet place that has no **distractions**—not even a window or a television.

3 Scientists believe that genetic mutations **underlie** a wide range of diseases and disorders.

4 Children who **display** aggressive or angry behavior in school may be having problems at home.

5 She said she would be arriving late. **Apparently**, a lot of flights have been delayed because of bad weather.

6 One of the **fundamental** principles of democracy is the freedom to express one's opinion freely.

7 The student's performance has been very **consistent**. She gets about 80% on most assignments and tests.

8 This study focuses **exclusively** on the behavior of children. Adults behave very differently and were investigated in a separate study.

a _____ (adj) basic, being the thing on which other things depend

b _____ (adv) limited to a specific thing, person, or group

c _____ (v) to be the cause of or a strong influence on something

d _____ (n) a movement of the body or a body part to express an idea or feeling

e _____ (n) something that prevents someone from giving full attention to something else

f _____ (adj) always behaving or happening in the same way

g _____ (adv) according to what seems to be true

h _____ (v) to show a feeling or attitude by what you say or do

THE PERFECT WORK TEAM

Getting the Best from a Group

1 For years, psychologists have known how to measure the intelligence of individuals, but only recently have they begun to investigate the issue of *group intelligence*. This notion stems from the observation that some groups seem to work well across tasks, even tasks that are not very similar. Early investigations suggest that group intelligence is not the sum of the intelligence of the individuals in it. So what is the secret to their success?

2 Researchers at Google and MIT have both tackled this question and they believe they finally have a handle on what makes some teams successful. In the Google study researchers amassed thousands of data points on hundreds of groups and combed through them trying to find patterns. Are the members of effective groups friends outside of work? Do groups whose members have similar personalities or backgrounds work together best? Does gender make a difference? They floated many theories but found no patterns to support them. In fact, *who* was in the group **apparently** did not seem to make a difference; instead, the difference between more and less effective groups seemed to lie in the interaction among the members.

3 The MIT group had already been gathering data on group interaction using digital "badges" that participants in the study agreed to wear. These badges provided a wealth of information, including how long people spoke and to whom, what kinds of gestures they made, where they were looking during interaction, and their facial expressions. As in the Google study, this research group concluded that the key to an effective team is how members interact.

> **"**
> **[S]ide conversations between individual members during meetings, far from being a distraction, actually increased the group's productivity.**

4 Among the findings, the most consistent and significant is that, in effective groups, members spoke for a roughly equal amount of time—not at every meeting or interaction, but across the course of a project. A second consistent finding was that members displayed empathy, an understanding of how it might feel to walk in someone else's shoes. This social sensitivity is measured by a relatively new test, called the "Reading the Mind in the Eyes." The test assesses individual differences in two key factors, social awareness and emotion recognition, by asking individuals to guess emotions based on only a picture of a person's eyes. High levels of these two features create what one of the researchers in the Google study calls psychological safety: Members of the group feel comfortable voicing their opinions and making suggestions without fear of a negative response from other members of the group, and they believe that others will listen to them and value what they say. When these conditions are present, the group as a whole tends to be effective.

5 There were additional findings that support these general ones. For example, in effective groups, members face one another directly when they speak, and they use energetic and enthusiastic gestures. They also communicate directly with one another, not just through the leader or manager of the group. In fact, the MIT study found that side conversations between individual members during meetings, far from being a **distraction**, actually increased the group's productivity. All the findings highlight the importance of having face-to-face meetings instead of phone calls, teleconferences, or email communications. The positive behaviors uncovered in these studies occur primarily or **exclusively** in face-to-face interaction. The MIT team estimates that 35% of a team's performance can be explained just by the number of their face-to-face exchanges.

6 One might argue that most of these findings are extremely obvious, and needless to say, good managers have probably always understood these principles. Our social and professional lives, however, are not always structured in ways that facilitate the kind of interaction that apparently underlies effective group performance. Understanding group intelligence can help businesses and other organizations make the fundamental changes necessary to improve group performance.

The Dream of the Videophone

In the 1960s and 1970s, TV shows about the future showed people using imagined technologies, such as flying cars and machines for getting dressed in the morning. Most dream technology remains just a dream. However, one futuristic dream gadget has come true—the videophone. In old science fiction, people of the future conversed while looking at each other on screens. It wasn't exactly like modern online video conversation via Skype, Zoom, or Hangout, but it was similar.

Videophoning had an advantage over other technologies: at the time it was being portrayed as futuristic, it already existed. Bell Labs set up videophone booths at the 1964 World's Fair in Queens, New York, where visitors could video-converse live with someone at Disneyland in California. After the fair, AT&T put these Picturephones on the market, but they never connected with many customers—probably because of extremely high costs. In a way, the videophone was waiting for the Internet. Now, to video-connect, users do not need to buy special equipment beyond a laptop, and they get basic connections free via Wi-Fi.

The quality of the communication has been another issue. The occasional dropped calls, the slow Wi-Fi, and the unflattering video images of basic video conversation are tolerable for simply keeping in touch with friends. But when big business or international diplomacy is on the line, video connections may not yet be a substitute for face-to-face communication. The videophone dream will truly be fulfilled only when technology can convey subtle clues of expression and tone without a 200-millisecond lag.

WHILE READING

4 READING FOR MAIN IDEAS Read the article on pages 164–166. Highlight the sentences that best express the main ideas of the article. Highlight no more than six sentences.

5 TAKING NOTES Read the article again. Complete the table with results from the MIT study about the characteristics of effective groups and their members.

major findings	1 equal speaking time
	2
additional findings	3
	4 gestures
	5
	6

6 SUMMARIZING Write a summary of the article. Use your notes in Exercise 4 and your responses to Exercise 5 to guide you. Remember that not every detail from exercise 5 belongs in your summary.

_____

_____

_____

_____

_____

_____

_____

7 Work with a partner. Compare your summaries from Exercise 6. Offer each other advice for improvement.

READING BETWEEN THE LINES

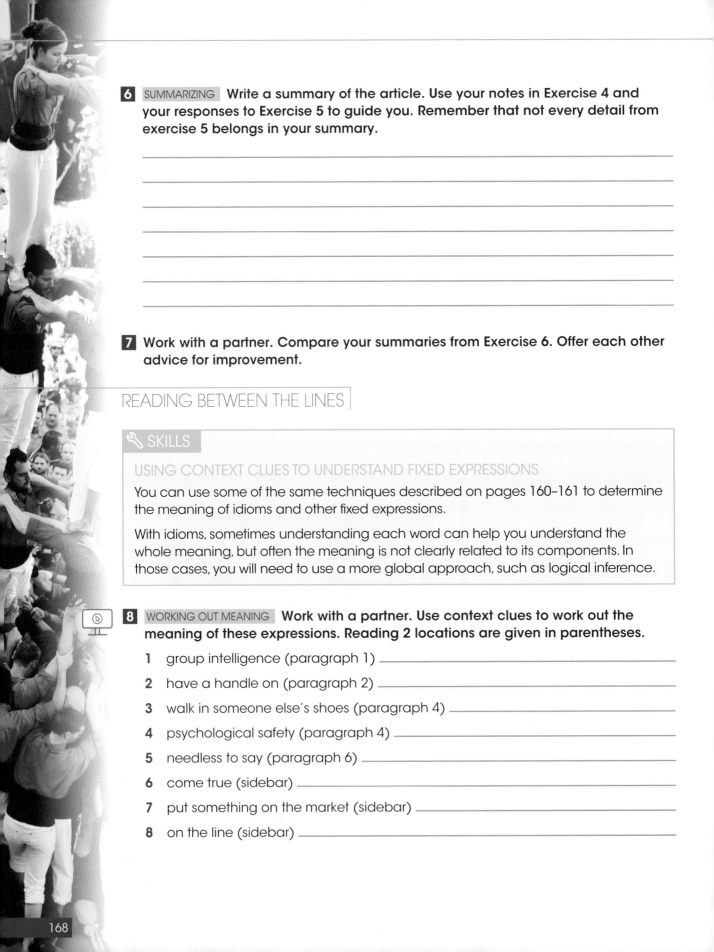

🔧 SKILLS

USING CONTEXT CLUES TO UNDERSTAND FIXED EXPRESSIONS

You can use some of the same techniques described on pages 160–161 to determine the meaning of idioms and other fixed expressions.

With idioms, sometimes understanding each word can help you understand the whole meaning, but often the meaning is not clearly related to its components. In those cases, you will need to use a more global approach, such as logical inference.

8 WORKING OUT MEANING Work with a partner. Use context clues to work out the meaning of these expressions. Reading 2 locations are given in parentheses.

1 group intelligence (paragraph 1) _____

2 have a handle on (paragraph 2) _____

3 walk in someone else's shoes (paragraph 4) _____

4 psychological safety (paragraph 4) _____

5 needless to say (paragraph 6) _____

6 come true (sidebar) _____

7 put something on the market (sidebar) _____

8 on the line (sidebar) _____

☼ CRITICAL THINKING

9 **Work with a partner to do a version of the test mentioned in Reading 2.**

UNDERSTAND	**ANALYZE**	**ANALYZE**
Look carefully but quickly at each set of eyes.	Choose the word that you think best describes how the person is feeling.	Compare your choices with those of your partner. Discuss the reasons for your choices.

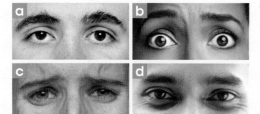

🗫 COLLABORATION

10 A Work in a small group. Conduct a real-life version of the eye test. Each person chooses two public settings where people can easily be observed in conversation - for example, a coffee shop, the library, or a student lounge.

B Observe five conversations in each setting. As you observe, be polite. Do not get too close, and do not listen in on any quiet conversations. If people seem uncomfortable as you watch them, stop and leave.

C Take notes. Include the name of the setting, general details about the people conversing, and a short description of their eye expressions. For example:

Setting: coffee shop, 8:15 a.m.

1: male barista – <u>cheerful, welcoming</u>; female customer – <u>uncertain, searching</u>

D Compare notes as a group. Discuss any patterns and explanations for those patterns. Then share your findings with the class.

LANGUAGE FOR HEDGING

LANGUAGE

In some forms of writing it is fine to make bold, unqualified claims and generalizations. In formal writing, however, writers need to make it clear that they understand that other viewpoints exist and have credibility. Formal writers do not often take absolute positions. Instead, they limit generalizations and hedge their claims to make them more modest—and as protection from accusations that their work is untrue or misleading.

Bold claim

Face-to-face interaction is the most effective form of communication.

Hedged claim

In most cases, face-to-face interaction is the most effective form of communication.

It has been suggested that face-to-face interaction is the most effective form of communication.

Face-to-face interaction **may / tends to** be the most effective form of communication.

Hedging devices

There are many ways to hedge or soften a claim.

Quantifiers and approximators
most / some / many

fairly / somewhat

often / usually

more or less

Adverbs and adverb phrases
for the most part

primarily

apparently

relatively

perhaps

typically

mainly

generally

in general

Modal verbs
can / could / may

Lexical verbs and phrases
tends

suggests

seems

appears

is likely to

Introductory phrases
There is evidence that

It appears / seems that

It has been suggested that

This indicates that

It may be the case that

It is (often) thought that

It is widely believed / assumed that

1 Rewrite these bold claims to make them more modest. Compare sentences with a partner.

1 Human error is the cause of traffic fatalities.

2 Lack of sleep leads to both emotional and physical problems.

3 If you know your personality type, you can find the job that is best for you.

4 Tall people make the best basketball players.

5 People who are obese will develop diabetes.

6 We will run out of fossil fuels in about 100 years.

2 Write three hedged statements of your own about building teams for effective collaboration.

1

2

3

WATCH AND LISTEN

GLOSSARY

indelible (adj)   impossible to remove by washing or any other method

mindset (n)   a person's way of thinking and their opinions

congregate (v)   to gather together into a large group

communal (adj)   belonging to or used by all members of a group

synergy (n)   the combined power of a group of things when they are working together that is greater than the total power achieved by each working separately

pull an all-nighter (v)   to stay awake all night studying or working on a project

one-upmanship (n)   an effort to show that you are better than someone else

rule with an iron fist (v)   to control a group of people very firmly, having complete power over everything they do

PREPARING TO WATCH

1 ACTIVATING YOUR KNOWLEDGE **Check (✓) the ideas you agree with. Discuss your choices with a partner.**

1   I prefer to work alone.   ☐

2   I like working in a quiet office environment.   ☐

3   I like working in an open space where I can hear others.   ☐

4   I would like to work for a company that encourages play.   ☐

5   I would like to work for a company that is flexible.   ☐

WHILE WATCHING

2 UNDERSTANDING MAIN IDEAS **Watch the video. Circle the correct answer.**

1   What does the informal workspace reduce?

   a   collaboration

   b   seriousness

   c   the need to meet people

2   Which of the following is **not** common at this creative company?

   a   working over 100 hours a week

   b   synergy between people

   c   scheduling a place to get work done

3   What does Carisa Bianci believe this type of workspace encourages?

   a   an employee's best performance

   b   competition from other companies

   c   relaxation

▶ **3** MAKING INFERENCES **Watch the video again. Work with a partner. Discuss the questions.**

   1   How do you think the employees feel about the space?

   2   Why do you think playing basketball is encouraged?

   3   Why do you think employees sometimes work over 100 hours a week?

☀ CRITICAL THINKING

4 Work with a partner. Discuss the questions.

APPLY	ANALYZE	EVALUATE
Would you like to work at a creative company like the one in the video? Why or why not?	Why do you think more and more offices are changing their culture?	Which is more valuable to a company, highly talented individuals or strong teamwork?

🐝 COLLABORATION

5 A Work in a small group. Imagine you are new employees at a start-up company that wants your input on workplace features for a creative, welcoming, productive work environment. Brainstorm a list of at least 10 features.

   B Discuss your ideas with another group. Agree on five features to present to the class. After all groups have presented their ideas and reasons, decide on the five most important features.

GLOSSARY OF KEY VOCABULARY

Words that are part of the Academic Word List are noted with Ⓐ in this glossary.

UNIT 1 CONSERVATION

READING 1

capacity Ⓐ (n) ability
deliberate (adj) intentional
emerge Ⓐ (v) to become known
memorabilia (n) a collection of items connected to a person or event
practice (n) a regular or widespread habit or behavior
prompt (v) to cause to do something
recover Ⓐ (v) to get something back
vulnerable (adj) not well protected; able to be harmed

READING 2

affordable (adj) not expensive
deteriorate (v) to grow worse
developers (n) companies that buy land and build on it
facility Ⓐ (n) a building for a special purpose
maintain Ⓐ (v) to continue to claim
prosper (v) to be successful
renovation (n) the repair of a building to bring it into good condition
vacant (adj) empty

UNIT 2 DESIGN

READING 1

appropriate Ⓐ (adj) correct or right for a particular situation
contemporary Ⓐ (adj) existing or happening now
criteria Ⓐ (n pl) standards used for judging something
devoted to Ⓐ (adj) for one particular purpose
donation (n) money or goods given to a person or organization in an attempt to help
human rights (n pl) fair and moral treatment that every person deserves
retain Ⓐ (v) to keep; to continue having
subsequent Ⓐ (adj) next; happening after something else

READING 2

appeal (to) (v) to be interesting or attractive (to)
associate (v) to make a connection in one's mind with
evolve Ⓐ (v) to develop slowly
modify Ⓐ (v) to change somewhat
opposition (to) (n) disagreement with
opt for (v) to choose
resemble (v) to look like
resist (v) to fight against

Answer to the puzzle on page 102.

UNIT 3 PRIVACY

READING 1

abusive (adj) bad and cruel; causing another person mental or physical harm

anonymous (adj) unidentified or unidentifiable

disturbing (adj) upsetting; causing worry

guarantee Ⓐ (v) to promise absolutely and legally

humiliation (n) shame and loss of self-respect

validity Ⓐ (n) reasonableness or acceptability

violate Ⓐ (v) to break, such as a law or agreement

withdraw (v) to stop participating

READING 2

assemble Ⓐ (v) to gather

barrier (n) something that blocks access

eliminate Ⓐ (v) to remove; to get rid of completely

malicious (adj) intentionally hurtful

penalty (n) punishment

prosecute (v) to take to court to determine the guilt of

regulate Ⓐ (v) to control

suspended Ⓐ (adj) not allowed to participate in an activity for a period of time

UNIT 4 BUSINESS

READING 1

aspiring (adj) wishing to become successful

break even (idm) to earn only enough money to pay expenses

component Ⓐ (n) one of the parts of something

fluctuate Ⓐ (v) to change frequently from one level to another

outweigh (v) to be greater or more important than something else

proposition (n) a proposal or suggestion, especially in business

revenue Ⓐ (n) the money that a business receives regularly

transition Ⓐ (n) a change from one state or condition to another

READING 2

accumulate Ⓐ (v) to gradually collect

attainable Ⓐ (adj) able to be reached

follow suit (v phr) to do the same thing

incentive Ⓐ (n) encouragement based on rewards

ongoing Ⓐ (adj) continuing

pioneer (n) one of the first people to do something

retention Ⓐ (n) holding; keeping

shrewdly (adv) based on good judgment

UNIT 5 PSYCHOLOGY

READING 1
intriguing (adj) very interesting; mysterious
label Ⓐ (v) to assign a (usually negative) characteristic to someone or something
norm Ⓐ (n) accepted standard or way of doing something
notion Ⓐ (n) idea
pursue Ⓐ (v) to continue or to try to do something over a period of time
reject Ⓐ (v) to refuse to accept
skeptical (adj) doubting that something is true
suppress (v) to prevent something from being expressed or known

READING 2
breakthrough (n) important discovery that helps solve a problem
confirm Ⓐ (v) to state or show that something is true
innovative Ⓐ (adj) new and different
procrastinator (n) a person who waits as long as possible to begin work
resourceful Ⓐ (adj) skilled at solving problems
seek Ⓐ (v) to try to find or get something
stimulation (n) something that arouses enthusiasm, curiosity, or activity
trigger Ⓐ (v) to cause something to happen or exist

UNIT 6 CAREERS

READING 1
alternative Ⓐ (adj) different from what is usual
assertive (adj) forceful; bold and confident
boast (v) to talk proudly about; to have or own something to be proud of
expertise Ⓐ (n) a high level of knowledge or skill
persistent Ⓐ (adj) strong and determined; lasting for a long time and difficult to resolve
prospective Ⓐ (adj) possible, especially in the future
qualified (adj) having the necessary knowledge or skill
survey Ⓐ (n) a set of questions asked of a large number of people in order to find patterns

READING 2
ambiguity Ⓐ (n) the state of being unclear or having more than one possible meaning
chronic (adj) lasting for a long time, especially something bad
diminish Ⓐ (v) to decrease in size or importance
dispute (v) to disagree with
extend (v) to go further, make bigger, or last longer
founder Ⓐ (n) someone who establishes an organization
illustration Ⓐ (n) an example that explains something
potential Ⓐ (n) the possibility to develop and succeed

UNIT 7 HEALTH SCIENCES

READING 1
bounce back (phr v) to return to normal
counter (v) to oppose; to defend against
cycle (A) (n) repeating series of events
grim (adj) very bad; worrisome
mild (A) (adj) not extreme
revolutionize (A) (v) to completely change
therapeutic (adj) healing; healthful
thrive (v) to live and develop successfully

READING 2
confine (A) (v) to exist in or apply to a limited group or area
detection (A) (n) the notice or discovery of something
domesticated (A) (adj) under human control; used for animals
eradicate (v) to get rid of something completely
facilitate (A) (v) to make something possible or easier
proximity (n) nearness
surge (n) a sudden, large increase
transmission (A) (n) the process of passing something from one person or place to another

UNIT 8 COLLABORATION

READING 1
accomplish (v) to do something successfully
coordinate (A) (v) to make separate things or people work well together
decline (A) (v) to worsen; to decrease
detract from (phr v) to make something worse or less valuable
differentiate (A) (v) to show or find the difference between one thing and another
enhance (A) (v) to improve
isolate (A) (v) to separate something from other connected things
phenomenon (A) (n) something that can be experienced or felt, especially something that is unusual or new

READING 2
apparently (A) (adv) according to what seems to be true
consistent (A) (adj) always behaving or happening in the same way
display (A) (v) to show a feeling or attitude by what you say or do
distraction (n) something that prevents someone from giving full attention to something else
exclusively (A) (adv) only; limited to a specific thing, person, or group
fundamental (A) (adj) basic, being the thing on which other things depend
gesture (n) a movement of the body or a body part to express an idea or feeling
underlie (A) (v) to be the cause of or a strong influence on something

VIDEO SCRIPTS

UNIT 1

Reporter: The CD is now a collector's item, replaced by digital downloads. But those who built up music libraries in the 80s and 90s may wonder, how long will those discs work—something Fenella France and her team are hoping to figure out.

Fenella France: You can see this one, it looks pretty good.

Reporter: Right.

France: And then this one.

Reporter: Oh my! France is the chief of preservation research and testing at the Library of Congress.

France: So we've kind of lost the entire reflective layer off of this one.

Reporter: Same CD?

France: Same CD.

Reporter: Produced at the same time.

Reporter: She and her colleagues are studying CDs like this one so they can better understand how to keep them safe for posterity. It turns out not all of the biggest challenges in preserving history involve documents that are centuries old.
One would think, oh, I need to worry about the parchment or the paper degrading, not the things from 20 years ago.

France: That's correct, and that's a challenge, I think. We've always focused on traditional materials, so to speak.

Reporter: How long a CD will last is not as simple as how old it is. Different manufacturers use different methods with vastly different results when it comes to durability.

France: We'd love to be able to say: these particular discs or this specific time, these are the absolute ones at risk. We don't know how people have stored or used them over time, so all of those factors—the use, the handling, the environment—all come into play in terms of the longevity.

Reporter: Which is where the idea of accelerated aging comes in. The CDs are actually cooked in these chambers, and by manipulating the humidity and the temperature, the discs can be aged a certain number of years.
The only thing that's different is how you've artificially aged them?

France: They were aged under the same conditions. One survived, one did not. So that's the challenge we have, that you never quite know how it's going to affect your CD.

Reporter: And if you want to preserve your CD collection at home, here's a few tips.

France: Probably don't put any nice fancy labels onto the top of CDs.

Reporter: And fair warning, you want to avoid those Sharpies.

France: There are some pens that they say don't cause any damage. There's a little piece in the center of the disc, and if you need to, just write on that center region.

Reporter: As for preserving the library's collection, France and her team plan to test the CDs every three to five years to make sure as little as possible is lost to history.

UNIT 2

Man: So, this is what I'm talking about. This is, uh, *Life* magazine, 1953. One ad after another in here—it just kind of shows every single visual bad habit that was, like, endemic in those days. You've got, uh, you know, zany hand lettering everywhere, this swash typography to kind of signify elegance. Exclamation points, exclamation points, exclamation points! Cursive wedding invitation typography down here reading, "Almost everyone appreciates the best." Uh, this was everywhere in the 50s. This is how everything looked in the 50s. You cut to, um—this is after Helvetica was in full swing, same product. No people, no smiling fakery. Just a beautiful, big glass of ice-cold Coke. The slogan underneath: "It's the real thing. Period. Coke. Period." In Helvetica. Period. Any questions? Of course not. Drink Coke. Period. Simple.

Leslie Savan: Governments and corporations love Helvetica because, on one hand, it makes them seem neutral and efficient; but also, it's the smoothness of the letters, makes them seem almost human. That is a quality they all want to convey because, of course, they have the image they're always fighting, that they are authoritarian, they're bureaucratic, you lose yourself in them, they're oppressive. So instead, by using Helvetica, they can come off seeming more accessible, transparent, and accountable.

UNIT 3

Gayle King (co-host): Now to the photo hacking scandal everybody's talking about. As we told you earlier, Apple now says those nude celebrity images were stolen in, quote, "… a very targeted attack on user names, passwords, and security questions …", adding that "None of the cases we have investigated has resulted from a breach in any of Apple's systems including iCloud® or Find my iPhone." The FBI is now on the case, so we wanted to look at the bigger implications of this. CBS news legal analyst Rikki Klieman joins us from Boston. Rikki, good morning to you.

Rikki Klieman: Good morning.

King: Hey, how is the FBI involved in the case? What exactly are they doing?

Klieman: Well, the FBI is going to look at all of the systems. Despite Apple saying that it really comes from the idea of "forgot your password," they will be looking at the devices belonging to these movie stars—that is, their mobile phones, their computers, their backup systems—and they will also then be searching to look for, in essence, the virtual fingerprints of the hackers themselves.

King: So who do you think could be charged here, the hackers, the websites? The people that posted the videos, the pictures?

Klieman: Well, you have to look from the greatest to the smallest. We know that the hackers can be charged. There's a law on the books as far back as 1986, and it's called the Computer Fraud and Abuse Act. And that's really the big law, because what we have there are penalties for each count, each hacking, and that goes to five years a count and even, with enhancements, it may be more than that. You may remember that there was a case where Scarlett Johansson among others, her nude photos were hacked. The person in Florida who did that, a man by the name of Christopher Chaney, he wound up with a 10-year plea on the basis of nine counts. So he could have gotten a lot more than that. What we look at after that is people who have put it on the website—it's the people who put it up there that may become liable, both criminally and civilly. The website's not going to be liable, and certainly the people who look at it are not going to be liable.

Norah O'Donnell (co-host): Can I ask you about— there are certainly a lot of headlines out there where people are saying, you know, this isn't just a scandal, it's a sex crime against these women.

Klieman: Well, it's not a sex crime against these women. Uh, the reality of this is, it is a computer crime and a computer crime only, despite the fact that it's this kind of public exposure of something that is really private. When we have something in our cell phone, we have a reasonable expectation of privacy, that no one is going to look at that. But it doesn't mean that by someone hacking into it and putting it out there that it is a sex crime. In fact, the worst part of all of this is—if I read one more thing about people blaming the victims in this case. If you take a photo in the privacy of your own home, with your husband, with your significant other, or all by yourself—and then let alone the fact that some of these photos were deleted—why, in heaven's name, do you expect that some hacker is going to go in there? That is not, it just is not a reasonable expectation of privacy. It is your own, and we shouldn't blame the victim.

Charlie Rose (co-host): Thank you so much, Rikki.

UNIT 4

Anna Werner (reporter): Willow Tufano may look like a typical teen, dress like one, and act like one, but growing up during Florida's foreclosure crisis gave her the opportunity to become something else, too.

Willow Tufano: I bought my first house and I'm buying my second house here soon.

Werner: You're a landlord?

Tufano: Yes.

Werner: She's likely Florida's youngest landlord, taking her cues from her realtor mom who buys cheap, bankowned homes.

Tufano: I would go around with my mom and look at these houses, and there was one that was filled with a whole bunch of furniture that was nice, and I said, well, I could sell this stuff. So that was how it started.

Werner: Willow eventually made $6,000 by selling furniture, which she used to help her purchase this $12,000 home. She'll soon close on her second house, this one. It costs $17,500.

Tufano: I'm trying to get as many houses as I can while the market is low.

Werner: What's your goal?

Tufano: I want to have probably around 10 houses by the time that I'm 18.

Werner: 10?

Tufano: Yes, I want to try for two a year, pretty much.

Werner: Today, Willow spends her spare time gathering and selling items not just from foreclosed homes but from garage sales, from charities, even street curbs.

Tufano: I just try and save every penny that I can to invest in more houses.

Werner: As a minor, Willow can't legally be on the deed. But when she turns 18, her mother, Shannon Moore, will sign the properties over to her.

Shannon Moore: I said, "Willow, lead the way. Show me where you need to go." And she has.

Werner: Not bad for a kid with attention deficit hyperactivity disorder who left a gifted school because teachers told her mom her daughter couldn't focus.

Moore: I guess it's hard to, you know, listen to people say your kid has a problem, you know. And then now look at her. I don't know, I guess I'm really proud of her.

Werner: These days Willow's busy collecting rent from her tenants, shopping for building materials, and taking stock of her next project.

Moore: I think that would work.

Werner: All from a girl who is too young to drive but has plenty of direction. Anna Werner, CBS News, North Port, Florida.

UNIT 5

Charlie Rose (co-host): For 30 years David Kelley and his brother Tom have taken familiar products and made them better. Their design firm IDEO reengineered everything from the computer mouse to television remote controls and even the classroom chair. Now the brothers have put out a new book. It is called *Creative Confidence: Unleashing the Creative Potential within All of Us* [sic]. David and Tom Kelley, welcome.

David and Tom Kelley: Thanks.

Rose: So what is creative confidence?

Tom Kelley: Well, it's really two things. It's the natural human ability to come up with breakthrough ideas combined with the courage to act on those ideas. Because, when we did a hundred interviews for the book, what we discovered is some people have the ideas but they—they have fear of being judged, and so they just hold it all in, and then their idea disappears. And so it's the—it's the ability to come up with the ideas but the courage, too.

Gayle King (co-host): And you both believe that everybody can be creative. I tell you, after looking at the book, I am thinking differently. You said *everybody*. I've never believed that.

David Kelley: Yeah, well, look at little kids in kindergarten.

King: Yes.

David Kelley: Everybody, you know, they're like, they're making like, uh, you know, a picture of a chicken with four legs, and mom puts it up on the refrigerator and says, "Yay!" So, we all have it in kindergarten, and somewhere along the line—

King: In fourth grade, you say.

David Kelley: Yeah, I think it's about fourth grade, you opt out and think of yourself as not creative because you're kind of being judged by your peers, or a teacher tells you that's not a very good drawing, or whatever. And it's just—it's just too bad.

Norah O'Donnell (co-host): I have young children and, you know, I see this happen early on in schools. They say, "Oh, that child is very creative," you know? And you get the assumption that people are born creative, and yet you do not believe that, as Gayle mentioned earlier. But you also think you can teach and continue to foster creativity.

David Kelley: Yeah, I mean, it's funny, you know. Somehow we have, sort of, *creativity* tied up with, kind of, *talent*, and it's really not the case. So, you know, you don't really expect a person to sit down at the piano and play for the first time. You know, like, that would be crazy. But we somehow think that either you can draw or you can't draw. You know, like, some—drawing takes just as much practice as playing the piano does and so, um, you find your different ways. You may be a creative curator. You

may be a creative person who, you know, figures things out in new ways and still can't draw. Right? But, so, creativity is—needs to be defined as the ability to, kind of, come up with new ideas in, kind of, unique ways. If you think about being creative, if you just take all the little parts of a project, what that adds to—and then you say, how can I make this little piece, you know, extraordinary? How can I make this little piece extraordinary?

King: For someone who is listening to you, what is the first thing we should do if we think, I'm not creative.

David Kelley: Yeah.

King: I want to be creative.

David Kelley: Yeah, so, get the book.

King: Other than that.

David Kelley: But the whole thing is—is getting in and building empathy for people. We find that—we see this thing called "bias towards action" where you jump right in. I mean, so many people spend time planning and think, I'm going to go. Instead, just jump in. If you're designing a new, you know, uh, bicycle, go out and watch people ride bicycles. Talk to people who don't ride bicycles. Ride a bicycle yourself. Go to the stores. I mean, all of that, we call it empathy. You're having empathy for the people. If I'm trying to please a certain person, I really want to build empathy for them. And I think it's, kind of, an underserved area. We mostly look at technology or business.

Rose: Yes.

David Kelley: And come up with those kind of ideas and then try to convince people to—that they might like it. It's much better, I believe, to go out and, like, really build empathy for people. What do they really want? What's meaningful to people is really where we go. If it's meaningful for people, then in some ways it's easier to go find technologies and business ideas that solve that particular problem.

UNIT 6

Nick Sinetti: I don't really dig the second shift, but you've got to start somewhere.

Reporter: Despite the worst job market in decades, listen to what 20-year-old Nick Sinetti found right out of high school. How many offers did you get?

Sinetti: Um, three, I think.

Reporter: Three offers?

Sinetti: Right.

Reporter: He graduated in 2009 as a certified welder from a career in technical education high school, or what used to be called vocational education. He now works for Air Products in Allentown, Pennsylvania. Of the 7,500 employees that you have here in the United States, how many are, what you would say, are the skilled workers?

John McGlade: 4,000.

Reporter: John McGlade is president and CEO of Air Products. His global company designs and builds hightech hydrogen equipment and devices. How worried are you that you won't find enough skilled workers in the future?

McGlade: I'm worried. I've been worried.

Reporter: McGlade says he hires about 550 U.S. workers a year—360 are technically skilled positions that require two years of college or advanced certification. These positions can often go unfilled for twelve months.

McGlade: You need people who are electronics experts, who are instrument technicians, who are mechanics that can work on today's modern equipment.

Reporter: But this year funding for vocational education was cut by $140 million, and President Obama is proposing a 20% cut next year. What is your, sort of, biggest fear if there isn't this continued support for vo-tech education?

McGlade: Without the support and without the continued development of the skilled workforce, um, we're not going to be able to fill the jobs.

Reporter: Lehigh Career and Technical Institute would be impacted as well. Five percent of its budget comes from federal grants.

Teacher: 24 divided by 1.5E, that tells us—

Reporter: The school trains about 3,000 students from across the Lehigh Valley. According to the National Association of Career and Technical schools, these students can earn about $26 an hour more than similar students in non-technical fields.

McGlade: There's going to be more and more of those skilled jobs available that are going to be well paying and be a sustainable career for years and years to come.

Reporter: A career path that McGlade estimates will need 10 million more skilled workers over the next decade.

UNIT 7

Tom Dukes: I never thought it would happen to me.

Katie Couric (reporter): Tom Dukes was the picture of health, an energetic 52-year-old sales executive in Lomita, California, who worked out four hours a day until late last year when he was rushed to the hospital in agonizing pain. An hour later he was on the operating table.

Dukes: I thought, you know, I might just be saying goodbye. That was my last thought.

Couric: Dukes awoke to a shocking reality. Surgeons had to repair a hole in his abdomen caused by a raging E. coli infection developed after eating contaminated meat. This form of E. coli was much more aggressive because it had several genetic mutations making it resistant to antibiotics.

Dukes: Everything was getting, you know, progressively worse quickly.

Couric: Duke's story concerns infectious disease doctors, like Brad Spellberg, author of *Rising Plague*.

Brad Spellberg: These organisms are the experts at resistance.

Couric: He says more infections are starting out as bacteria in food or other ordinary places and evolving into deadly, drug-resistant superbugs.

Spellberg: It is starting to move out of the hospitals and into the communities.

Couric: And what happens to those people?

Spellberg: We're at a point where we may have to start admitting tens of thousands of women with simple urinary tract infections to the hospital.

Couric: Because that infection has outsmarted the pills?

Spellberg: Yep. Because the E. coli that causes most urinary tract infections is becoming resistant.

Couric: Health officials say that resistance is growing, especially among these five deadly bacteria. Virtually all of them carry genes that prevent antibiotics from working, and these genetic mutations are spreading. Another reason for these lethal strains—the overuse of antibiotics. A recent study finds more than 60% of antibiotics prescribed are unnecessary.

John Rex: It's a crisis that touches every country on the globe, touches people of all socioeconomic classes, all races.

Chemist: This represents the compounds that we're making—

Couric: John Rex is the head of drug development for AstraZeneca—one of only a few pharmaceutical companies still devoting resources for new medicines to cure these lethal bugs.

Rex: The trick is to find something that kills the bacteria but doesn't hurt you or me.

Couric: Developing a new antibiotic takes at least ten years and costs as much $1.7 billion. Drug companies make more money creating medicines people take every day for chronic conditions like high blood pressure, insomnia, or sexual dysfunction. Do you consider this a grave public health crisis?

Spellberg: Yeah. This is a convergence of two public health crises skyrocketing antibiotic resistance and dying antibiotic development.

Dukes: I was extremely fatigued. I was mentally exhausted.

Couric: It took four months and several drugs for Tom Dukes to finally beat his infection, but he says he'll never completely recover.

Dukes: I think about it every day because if it hadn't worked, I wouldn't be here.

UNIT 8

Carisa Bianci: The company is an advertising agency, but we like to think of ourselves as a creative company. So I think the space was designed to just allow creative thoughts and thinking.

Carol Madonna: Our architect was really smart. He provided us with really indelible materials. We have a thousand 27-year-olds here. They are pretty hard on stuff.

Jayanta Jenkins: The space in itself is designed for collaboration, so I think the mindset just, kind of, you know, very, sort of, fluidly flows that way here.

Jason Clement: I think we really have created this, uh, sense of a city in here where you really have what you need. You know, places where we congregate. We have places where we go away. There are communities, so we're organized by, you know, different projects and different work streams. So, you know, you get a sense of going from, you know, one part of town to another part of town.

Bianci: Main Street is where the creatives are, so all the square boxes there and the three layers of that, that's, kind of, Main Street.

Clement: You can get to the other side of the building by really walking across almost like a catwalk.

Jenkins: The part where we're sitting is a communal space where people can gather to talk about meetings, to go over client reviews, to have lunch.

William Esparza: When it comes to work, it just eliminates the seriousness, you know, and so you can start having ideas and have synergy happen between people informally.

Clement: But you can get work done without having to feel this formality, right, of needing to schedule time or needing to schedule a place to be able to get it done.

Bianci: People can pull over 100 hours a week. Um, it's—it's not uncommon. If you're in a new business pitch, you do a lot of all-nighters. You'll come here on the weekends and there's quite a few cars in the parking lot. You come back the next day, and they're wearing the same outfit that they have. So I think there're spaces here that people can, kind of, crash. Um, there's a whole dog community here.

Clement: Dogs add a lot to a meeting, right, in terms of just humanizing it. I think we can really have really tough meetings. We can disagree on things, and if a meeting is particularly tough and somebody starts licking your ankle, it really changes your tone.

Bianci: We tend to do basketball games as well. After hours you're going to see people running up and down that court.

Clement: Everybody shows up and we can get together as a family and share good news and sometimes bad news.

Bianci: I think, you know, whenever someone sees something that they respect and admire, you know, it gives them that, kind of like, all right, you know, I'm going to go and I'm going to, like, take it on, and I want to deliver something as good or better. It's a healthy competitiveness.

Esparza: Whether it's the Gatorade team or the Pepsi team, there's a sense of one-upmanship. You know, you want to make the best work out of the building.

Jenkins: The thing that isn't so nice about an open office plan sometimes is people can always walk in, but if you're really working and don't want to be interrupted, uh, it's nice to find areas in the building where you can see people but they can't see you. You can easily get a lot of work done where people wouldn't be able to find you unless, you know, you decided that you wanted to be found.
Right up above here is this billboard that has one of the Pepsi, um, adverts that we did, and right behind it is the perfect hiding place.

Madonna: We're nurturing everybody and helping them, you know, flourish here, but we also rule with an iron fist.

Text Credits

Graphs on pp. 117 Bureau of Labor Statistics; Graph on p. 120 adapted from Manpower Group "2016/2017 Talent Shortage Survey." Copyright © Manpower Group. Reproduced with kind permission; Graphs on p. 127 adapted from *Education at a Glance 2016: OECD Indicators*, OECD Publishing, Paris. DOI: http://dx.doi.org/10.1787/eag-2016-en. Copyright © 2016 OECD. Reproduced with kind permission; Figure on p. 139 adapted from "Clinical Microbiology Reviews: Challenges of Antibacterial Discovery" by Lynn L. Silver. Copyright © 2011 American Society for Microbiology. Reproduced with permission; Graphs on p. 159 adapted from "The Too-Much-Talent Effect: Team Interdependence Determines When More Talent Is Too Much or Not Enough" by Roderick I. Swaab, Michael Schaerer, Eric M. Anicich, Richard Ronay and Adam D. Galinsky. Copyright © SAGE Publications Ltd.

Photo Credits

The publishers are grateful to the following for permission to reproduce copyright photographs and material

Key: T = Top, C = Center, B = Below, L = Left, R = Right, TL = Top Left, TR = Top Right, BL = Below Left, BR = Below Right, CL = Center Left, CR = Center Right, BG = Background

pp. 38-39: IKEA; p. 39 (TC): FedEx; p. 39 (CL): World Wildlife Fund; p. 39 (CR): Human Rights; p. 47 (T): NBC; p. 47 (B): BP; p. 48 (T): Spotify; p. 48 (B): Tropicana; p. 79: Ira Berger/Alamy Stock Photo;

The following images are sourced from Getty Images.

pp. 14-15: Art by Mandy/Moment; p. 17: Bibikoff/E+; pp. 18-19: Alan Tunnicliffe Photography/Moment; p. 19: Mark Horn/Stone; p. 20: Franz45/DigitalVision Vectors; p. 23: Ivanastar/iStock; p. 24: Eyecrave/iStock; pp. 25-26: Johner Images; p. 27 (CR): English Heritage/Heritage Images; p. 27 (BR): Hufton + Crow/Corbis Documentary; p. 30: Education Images/Universal Images Group; p. 32: Jurgen Vogt/The Image Bank; pp. 34-35: Richard Newstead/Moment; p. 36 (TR): Andrew Dieb/Icon Sportswire; p. 36 (B): Alan Smith/Icon Sportswire; pp. 40-41: Bauhaus1000/iStock; p. 43: Alexander Spatari/Moment; p. 47: Dave/Les Jacobs/Blend Images; pp. 44-45: Tuomas Lehtinen/Moment; p. 49: Yuri_Arcurs/DigitalVision; p. 52: Andrew Hetherington/Stone; p. 54-55: PeopleImages/E+; p. 57: Skynesher/E+; p. 58 (spot): Matthew Horwood; pp. 58-59: Andree Frischkorn/EyeEm; p. 59: Siphotography/iStock; p. 60: Tom Grill/JGI/Blend Images; p. 63: Necdet Yilmaz/Anadolu Agency; p. 62: Blackregis/iStock; p. 65 (B): MacXever/iStock; pp. 64-65: Dong Wenjie/Moment; p. 67: South_agency/E+; p. 66: Dimitri Otis/Stone; p. 68: GODS_AND_KINGS/iStock; p. 71 (BL): Redhumv/E+; p. 71 (BR): Sergei Bobylev/TASS; p. 72: Monty Rakusen/Cultura; pp. 74-75: Lisegagne/E+; p. 77: Maica/E+; p. 76 (TR): Effrey Greenberg/Universal Images Group; p. 76 (CR): Matt Cardy; pp. 78-79: Kulakova; p. 80: Maskot; p. 83 (spot): Andresr/iStock; p. 83:

TriggerPhoto/E+; p. 84: Martin Barraud/OJO Images; p. 85 (TR): Imilian/iStock; p. 85 (BR): Trinette Reed/Blend Images; p. 87: Kevin Cruff; p. 88: Paul Bradbury/Caiaimage; p. 89: Jaap Arriens/NurPhoto; p. 91: Hero Images; p. 92: Nycshooter/iStock; pp. 94-95: Jeremy Sutton-Hibbert; p. 97: Rick Madonik/Toronto Star; p. 98 (B): Imagno/Hulton Archive; p. 98 (T): Warrenrandalcarr/iStock; p. 99: Joe Klamar/Afp; p. 100: Pixel_Pig/E+; p. 102 (TL): Suparat Malipoom/EyeEm; p. 102 (TC): Don Farrall/Photodisc; p. 102 (TR): Lawrence Manning; p. 104: Donald Iain Smith/Blend Images; p. 105: Erik Tham; p. 106: Michael Ochs Archives; p. 106 (BG): James Leynse; p. 107: Klaus Vedfelt/Iconica; p. 110: Fmajor/E+; p. 112: JFCreatives/Cultura Exclusive; pp. 114-115: Lucidio Studio, Inc./Moment; p. 117: Francis Dean/Corbis; p. 116: Daniel Acker/Bloomberg; pp. 119-120-121: D3sign/Moment; p. 121 (TL): Arne Hodalic/Corbis Documentary; p. 121 (TR): Monty Rakusen/Cultura; p. 120: Monty Rakusen/Cultura; pp. 124-125: Steve Dunwell/The Image Bank; p. 126: PeopleImages/E+; p. 131: Pixsooz/iStock; p. 132: Sam Edwards/Caiaimage; pp. 134-135: Amesy/E+; pp. 136-137: Urs Flueeler/EyeEm; p. 137 (flu): Ian Cuming/Ikon Images; p. 137 (lavender): Rod Edwards/VisitBritain; p. 137 (mosquito): Sinclair Stammer/Science Photo Library; p. 137 (antibiotics): Fahroni/iStock; p. 137 (bacteria): Jaruno11/iStock; p. 138: Reptile8488/E+; p. 139 (BR): BSIP/Universal Images Group; p. 139 (CR): Burazin/Photographer's Choice RF; p. 139 (TR): Alan Hopps/Moment Open; p. 142: Anankkml/iStock; p. 146 (CR): TacioPhilip/iStock; p. 146 (TR): David McNew; p. 144: Tim Graham News; p. 146 (BR): Jordan Lye/Moment; p. 147: ThamKC/iStock; p. 148 (TR): Esther Kok/EyeEm; p. 148 (BR): Tetra images; p. 152: Kateryna Kon/Science Photo Library; pp. 154-155: Geber86/E+; p. 157: Tom Ang/Photolibrary; pp. 158-159: Barry Chin/The Boston Globe; p. 159 (spot): AdShooter/E+; p. 162: Joshua Bright/The Washington Post; pp. 164-165: Grass-lifeisgood/Moment; p. 165: Kelvin Murray/Taxi; p. 167: Steve Chenn; p. 168: Guillem Lopez/Aurora; p. 169 (a): Lisa kimberly/Moment; p. 169 (b): LuminaStock/Vetta; p. 169 (c): Cary Wolinsky/Aurora; p. 169 (d): Darren Robb/Taxi; p. 169 (B): Sean Justice/UpperCut Images; p. 171: Dave/Les Jacobs; p. 172: Gary Burchell/DigitalVision.

We are grateful to the following companies for permission to use copyright logos:
p. 38: IKEA; p. 39: FedEx, World Wildlife Fund, Human Rights; p. 44; NBC, BP; p. 45: Spotify, Tropicana.

Video Supplied by BBC Worldwide Learning.

Video Stills Supplied by BBC Worldwide Learning.

Corpus

Development of this publication has made use of the Cambridge English Corpus (CEC). The CEC is a multi-billion word computer database of contemporary spoken and written English. It includes British English, American English, and other varieties of English. It also includes the Cambridge Learner Corpus, developed in collaboration with the University of Cambridge ESOL Examinations. Cambridge University Press has built up the CEC to provide evidence about language use that helps produce better language teaching materials.

Cambridge Dictionaries

Cambridge dictionaries are the world's most widely used dictionaries for learners of English. The dictionaries are available in print and online at dictionary.cambridge.org. Copyright © Cambridge University Press, reproduced with permission.

Typeset by QBS

Audio by John Marshall Media

INFORMED BY TEACHERS

Classroom teachers shaped everything about *Prism*. The topics. The exercises. The critical thinking skills. Everything. We are confident that *Prism* will help your students succeed in college because teachers just like you helped guide the creation of this series.

Prism Advisory Panel

The members of the *Prism* Advisory Panel provided inspiration, ideas, and feedback on many aspects of the series. *Prism* is stronger because of their contributions.

Gloria Munson
University of Texas, Arlington

Kim Oliver
Austin Community College

Wayne Gregory
Portland State University

Julaine Rosner
Mission College

Dinorah Sapp
University of Mississippi

Christine Hagan
George Brown College/Seneca College

Heidi Lieb
Bergen Community College

Stephanie Kasuboski
Cuyahoga Community College

GLOBAL INPUT

Teachers from more than 500 institutions all over the world provided valuable input through:
- Surveys
- Focus Groups
- Reviews